Routledge Revivals

THE FINALITY
OF THE
HIGHER CRITICISM

THE FINALITY
OF THE
HIGHER CRITICISM

OR

The Theory of Evolution and False Theology

BY

WILLIAM B. RILEY, D. D.

First published by HardPress Publishing

This edition first published in 2018 by Routledge
2 Park Square, Milton Park, Abingdon, Oxon, OX14 4RN
and by Routledge
52 Vanderbilt Avenue, New York, NY 10017, USA

Routledge is an imprint of the Taylor & Francis Group, an informa business

© Taylor and Francis

All rights reserved. No part of this book may be reprinted or reproduced or utilised in any form or by any electronic, mechanical, or other means, now known or hereafter invented, including photocopying and recording, or in any information storage or retrieval system, without permission in writing from the publishers.

Publisher's Note
The publisher has gone to great lengths to ensure the quality of this reprint but points out that some imperfections in the original copies may be apparent.

Disclaimer
The publisher has made every effort to trace copyright holders and welcomes correspondence from those they have been unable to contact.
A Library of Congress record exists under ISBN:

ISBN 13: 978-0-367-17992-2 (hbk)
ISBN 13: 978-0-367-17993-9 (pbk)
ISBN 13: 978-0-429-05894-3 (ebk)

ISBN: 9781290814669

Published by:
HardPress Publishing
8345 NW 66TH ST #2561
MIAMI FL 33166-2626

Email: info@hardpress.net
Web: http://www.hardpress.net

THE FINALITY
OF THE
HIGHER CRITICISM

―― OR ――

The Theory of Evolution and False Theology

―― BY ――

WILLIAM B. RILEY, D. D.
Pastor The First Baptist Church
MINNEAPOLIS

*Author of "Vagaries and Verities," "The Perennial Revival,"
"Messages for the Metropolis," etc.*

A FOREWORD.

IN publishing a volume, one should have a very definite object to accomplish. Our purpose in putting forth "The Finality of the Higher Criticism" will appear to its every reader.

We confess to a conscious call in this publication, being fully persuaded that the honor of Christ and the very life of His church are alike endangered by the doubting spirit now brooding over the educational institutions of America. Is it not high time the conservative and constructive ministers of our country united forces for the successful defense of "the faith once delivered?"

W. B. RILEY.

TABLE OF CONTENTS.

    I. The Higher Criticism According to Higher Critics.

   II. The Prominence of Skepticism in our Schools.

  III. The Prevalence of Skepticism in our Pulpits.

  IV. The Theory of Evolution and False Theology.

   V. The Sacred Scriptures—Are they Scientific?

  VI. Fosterism—Or the Finality of the Higher Criticism.

 VII. R. J. Campbell's Definition of the New Theology.

VIII. Skepticism—Is Satan Actually Back of It?

  IX. The True Scientific Spirit in Scripture Study.

   X. What will be the Religion of the Future?

Chapter I.

THE HIGHER CRITICISM ACCORDING TO HIGHER CRITICS.

"O Timothy, guard that which is committed unto thee, turning away from the profane babblings and oppositions of the knowledge which is falsely so-called; which some professing, have erred concerning the faith." (1 Tim. 6:20). This is Paul's advice to Timothy, his son and colaborer in the Gospel. Pretty nearly two thousand years have passed since the Apostle penned these words, and yet they are so pertinent that the conservative Senior in the Gospel ministry needs not to change one word when warning his Junior against the skepticism of those present-day scholars who assume to criticize the Sacred Scriptures. It would be difficult to conceive a more accurate description of the character and custom of our self-named Critics, than is found in this text.

It is our purpose in this address to give some time to the consideration of Skepticism and the

Scholars, and we prefer to be specific, dealing with individual scholars whose names are well-known, and whose positions, while unquestionably critical, are not so radical as to cause repudiation by their own brethren.

As a lad, hunting in the South, when a flock of quails rose before me, I always shot at the flock, and was greatly mystified that I so seldom hit anything. Later, I learned to pick out my bird, and discovered, to my surprise, that it was easier to hit one than it was all of them. Admiral Togo, in his naval engagement with Rojestventsky, illustrated the advantage of selecting a target. His order was that the ships should be sunken one at a time; and the wisdom appeared in the victory won.

Recently two men, each of whom proudly assumes the title "Higher Critic," have combined their pens in putting forth a booklet entitled "The Higher Criticism," in which they assume to instruct the public regarding their science, and to show its right to universal consideration, and the comparative certainty of its eventual adoption. I speak of R. S. Driver, Regius Professor of Hebrew at Oxford, and A. F. Kirkpatrick, who formerly held the same office in Cambridge. That these men are fairly content with this putting of the Higher Critic's position is evident in the fact that the booklet has passed through a number of editions.

As capable and conservative representatives of the school to which they belong, we propose the consideration of their statements concerning "The Higher Criticism" in the light of our text.

Paul's first requirement of Timothy is this—

"GUARD THE SACRED SCRIPTURES."

If one runs through his epistles he will discover that Paul regarded nothing else "committed" to the Gospel ministry, comparable to "the oracles of God." Writing to the Romans, he speaks of the advantages the Jews enjoyed "because that unto them were committed the oracles of God" (Romans 3:2). Writing to the Corinthians he recognizes the necessity of "delivering that which he had also received," namely, the statements of the Scriptures (1 Cor. 15:3-4). In his epistle to Titus (1:3) he affirms that "God had in due times manifested His word through preaching, which was now "committed unto him" according to the command of God our Saviour. It is not likely, therefore, that he has else in mind than the same sacred oracles, when he enjoins Timothy to "guard that which is committed" unto him. His injunction to Timothy is equally binding on the present Gospel ministry.

At what points do we need to guard the Sacred Scriptures?

1. *At the point of the truth about their text.* We consent with Messrs. Driver and Kirkpatrick that "the aim of the Christian student is truth." Let us have truth *versus* error; fact *versus* fiction; science *versus* speculation. Conservatives ask for no special privileges in such a contest; for no compromise in that conflict.

To the conflict then! These scholars say of the text of the sacred Scripture, "It is seriously corrupt." ("The Higher Criticism," p. 5.) We make bold to affirm that such a claim is without scientific confirmation. Twenty-one hundred years ago the text of the Old Testament was in every essential respect what it is at this hour, as one will discover who consults the Greek translation of that time. And, back of that day greater care was exercised in the translation of the text than has been shown by modern students. It was the unerring law, among the ancient priests and scribes to regard the slightest defect sufficient to vitiate the synagogue roll; even though it were but the blurring of the letters, brought about by the reverent kissing of the same, it resulted in the condemnation of the document. No less an authority than Prof. Sayce affirms it as a fact that the most minute care was bestowed upon the accuracy of the text;

and the work was done with such "scrupulous honesty" that in 1,500 years copies of one volume revealed differences but slight and unimportant. Those unquestioned scientists, in the whole realm of Sacred Scripture—Doctors Westcott and Hort—assert that of the many manuscripts gathered from all over the world, written on cloth, skin, parchment, papyrus, they did not essentially differ one from another in more than one word in a thousand. When one is made familiar with this fact, he is convinced that our critics have "strained at a gnat and swallowed a camel."

2. *As to the claims of Authorship.* Our scholarly brethren—Driver and Kirkpatrick—tell us (p. 6) "Hicher Criticism has investigated the origin of the various books," and they announce the result, page 20, "The historical books are now seen to be not, as was once supposed, the works (for instance) of Moses, or Joshua, or Samuel, but are compiled out of the writings of distinct and independent authors, characterized by different styles and representing different points of view, which were combined together and otherwise adjusted, till they finally assumed their present form."

Is that the truth? The science of Archeology contradicts the assertion. The Scriptures name these very men, Moses, Joshua and Samuel, as among their authors; and every turn of the spade is giving fresh confirmation to their claims. The very arguments once made against this authorship are now abandoned by the critics themselves. But yesterday they were affirming that writing was not sufficiently developed in Moses' day to make it possible for him to be the author of the Pentateuch. Discoveries drove them from that position; and now they claim that if Moses did write anything at all, he borrowed it in the main from his predecessors to have his productions improved and redacted. This reminds one of Esop's fable of the wolf, who threatened the lamb because he fed in his pasture. When the poor little thing maintained that he had never tasted grass, his mother's milk having sufficed, the wolf then charged him with drinking from his spring. That accusation being answered after the same manner, he fell upon him, saying, "Anyhow I will not be cheated out of my meal."

The Bible seems to be the only literary structure the world has yet produced after the plan of the Cathedral at Milan, requiring generations of workers and many centuries in laying its foundations, perfecting its walls and completing its cupolas. Men have long been surprised that the name of the original architect of Milan's Cathedral should have been lost, but have not disputed that Amadeo was the author of many of its most beautiful designs, nor yet that Tibaldi conceived the ornamentation of doors and windows, while Napoleon saw to its finishing touches. But here we have a literary cathedral beside which every other output of mind and pen pales as the stars fade before the rising sun. Yet the scholars would have us believe that not only is the original architect an unknown one, but that scarcely a man who wrought upon its foundations or finial can be certainly named. If that be true, it is the strangest circumstance of all human history.

We are familiar with the story of how, after the repulse of the great Persian invader, Greece enacted a law that no one, under penalty of death, should espouse art, except free men. On one day all Greece was at Athens to behold an exhibit in the Agora. Pericles presided, with Aspasia at his side; while Phidias, Socrates, Sophocles and others acted as judges. A group far more beautiful than the rest challenged universal attention, and excited the envy of all artists. But to the herald's repeated question, "Who is the sculptor of this group?" there came no answer, and the conviction settled upon them that it must be the product of a slave. Amid the commotion, a beautiful maiden, with torn dress and disheveled hair, was dragged into the Agora, and the officers cried as they came, "This woman knows the sculptor." To all their questions Cleone was silent. She knew that if she should speak she sealed her brother's doom. When Pericles could get nothing from her, he said, "The law is imperative; take the maiden to the dungeon." A youth, with emaciated face and flowing hair rushed from his hiding place and cried, "Oh, Pericles, forgive and save the maiden. She is my sister. The group is the work of my hands, and I am but a slave." The crowd cried out, "To the dungeon with him." But Pericles answered, "No, behold that group! Apollo decides by it that there is something higher in Greece than an unjust law. The highest purpose of law should be the development of the beautiful. If Athens lives in the memory and affections of men, it is her devotion to art that will immortalize her. Not to the dungeon, but to my side bring the youth." And that day the youth was crowned by Aspasia's hand and his name immortalized. He had wrought so great a work, that with the utmost care he could not escape detection. The work itself compelled the knowledge of him and created a place in history for him.

If the conclusion of the scholars from whom I have quoted is correct, we face this strangest fact of history, namely, that men, the authors of such institutions, such laws, and such a religion as the world has never known beside, the men who accomplished a work that only gods might ever be expected to complete, did it, and disappeared, leaving no name behind, not a footprint by which we can trace them to their homes; and this escape was accomplished without an endeavor. Such fictitious characters as Moses, Joshua, Samuel and David they have immortalized, and while about it, effected, forever, a personal oblivion! What thinking man can believe it?

The genius of DaVinci was such that his name is immortalized. Was he not musician, poet, sculptor and scientist in one? How could men forget him? And yet, strangely enough, the scholarship of a Driver and Kirkpatrick insists that the man who was the author of a Pentateuch —a marvel in letters, an unequalled genius in organization, a statesman of the highest order, a prophet whose vision swept the unborn centuries, dropped out of history and left neither sepulcher that can be known, nor residence that can be determined, nor name that can be called? Michael Angelo combined the ability of a great poet with the art of a peerless painter, and the achievements of an incomparable architect. No wonder men remember him! But the men who wrote the Psalms and Prophets gave us better poetry still, painted more lasting pictures, gave form to more permanent figures, and design to more abiding structures, and yet they are unknown, if Professors Driver and Kirkpatrick are to be accepted. Who believes it? Only he who is more anxious to secure the cheap reputation of standing with the scholarly than to search the pages of history and investigate the conclusions of so-called science.

3. *Concerning the historicity of recorded events.* The same gentlemen, on page 6 of "The Higher Criticism," say: "Historical Criticism affirms that much of the history has been colored by the beliefs and practices of the times in which the books were compiled, long after the event, and must be regarded as rather an ideal, than an actual picture of national life." And again, page 24, "In the early chapters of Genesis we are not reading literal history," while on page 29 they speak of "Scripture history" as having been "gradually shaped" into its present form by "tradition."

Perhaps it is not an impertinent question, "What other kind of history is there beside literal history!" Are fiction and fable history? Was not A. J. F. Behrends right when he spoke of idealized history as "idealized nonsense?" When Mr. Ingersoll was alive he often spoke of "The mistakes of Moses," to the delectation of a shabby, sinful, and shouting crowd. But have our scholars gone the great infidel one better, and made it out that Moses is a mistake; that he had no existence other than that of some creative imagination; that Jonah was little more a real man than was some hero of Ade's "Stories of the Streets and Town," or Mark Twain's "Innocents Abroad?" If scholars reach such conclusions, let them not insult our intelligence by turning back to us to say "But all this renders the Bible no less the Word of God." (See "The Higher Criticism," p. 8), When we have no better basis of inspiration than is found in pure fiction and distorted facts, honesty demands that we fling from us the volume that, claiming to be a Bible, can furnish no character and presents no more rational claims. But, fortunately, the statement of these gentlemen is not the shibboleth of all scholarship. Prof. Ira Price, the noted archæologist, reminds us "that remains of all the principal peoples mentioned in the Old Testament now decorate the cases of our museums, and tons of new material are being gathered in at the end of every season." He remarks, "These records, chiseled in adamantine volumes, stamped in perishable clay, painted in the darkness of the tombs, or cut on the mountain side, bring impartial, unimpeachable and conclusive proof of the veracity of the Old Testament."

Paul's injunction to Timothy is this—

AVOID THE FALSE SCHOLARSHIP.

"Guard that which is committed unto thee, turning away from the profane babblings and oppositions of the knowledge, which is falsely so-called." In reading and re-reading "The Higher Criticism" we have carefully inquired after the marks of "false scholarship" and have found three, manifesting themselves in this single production.

Such scholarship is self-assertive. It lays unwarranted claim to accomplishments. It does not hesitate to braggartly make mention of its "assured results," in the very same breath by which it has disputed the most sacred claims of Scripture. Some of us thought Mrs. Eddy slightly egotistical when she claimed that her writings were "divine and apodictical," and slightly self-assertive when she mentioned her own book ahead of the Bible, as essential to the education and redemption of the earth. But our Higher Critics contend with her for the chief seat in the synagogue of self-esteem. On one page our authors hesitate not to say concerning the Bible, "We must no longer talk of its infallibility and its inaccuracy" (p. 12); and on another they remind us of *"the assured results of criticism."* From their standpoint the whole field of so-called Revelation, from Genesis, 1:1 to Revelation 22:21, "is filled with temporary and imperfect elements," (p. 12), while they modestly (?) admit that their well-cultivated farm of "assured results" has a little "fringe of uncertainty," (p. 40), and that, mark you, as a result of "the imperfection or of the ambiguity of their data." (p. 41). Dr. P. S. Henson—Boston's inimitable orator—confesses that in his early youth, he was constantly distressed as to how the world would go on in case he died; but admits that maturity relieved him of that concern. There is no indication in "The Higher Criticism" that Brethren Driver and Kirkpatrick have yet escaped apprehension upon this same point, for since their scholarly research has produced results so much more "sure" than those of the ancient Scriptures, it would seem that a premature death on the part of one, or both of them, might even yet leave the world in uncertain light.

A second mark of false-scholarship is seen in its *self-contradiction.* On page 10 of "The Higher Criticism" one reads. "It is ridiculous to imagine that history can be re-written by the aid of a long series of unsupported guesses, however ingenious," while on page 36, after affirming the inspiration of the divine writers, they explain their history-making as follows: "In dealing with the earlier period in which no sure historical recollections reached back, they are dependent doubtless upon popular oral tradition. But penetrated, as they were, by deep moral and religious ideas, and possessing profound spiritual sensibilities, they so fill in the outlines, furnished by tradition, that the events or personages of antiquity become spiritually significant, embody spiritual lessons, or become spiritual types." A wag once remarked that his chief objection to lying was that it required such a good memory to make his after tales hang together. Not all of the self-styled scholars of the century have been blessed with this mental trait of good memory. R. F. Horton, one of the conservative higher critics of the old world, once delivered the Yale Lectures. One day he said, (Verbum Dei, p. 106), "All the great poets, from Homer and Hesiod down to Browning and Walt Whitman utter, in the stress of their poetic afflatus, truths and feelings which we can only explain by attributing them to God Himself. Even those who have stained their white-winged robes and thrown their heavenly crown in the dust, if they are real poets, will utter things which are as truly from God as the words of Balaam or the words of the faithless prophet that spake against the altar at Bethel. Goethe as a man seems more Hellenic than Christian; but Goethe as a poet has said things which we can only gratefully acknowledge come from God." Three days later, in lecturing on "The Preacher's

Personality," Mr. Horton remarked, "I have certainly spoken in vain, unless you are prepared to admit that while God may undoubtedly speak to men in many ways, and without any human intervention at all, He will not, even if He could, use evil men to be the ministrants of His Word. As in the old external covenant they must be pure who bare the vessels of the Lord, so in the spiritual society of Christ— no man can see God unless he is pure in heart; and no man can either receive, or deliver, the Word of God unless he is inwardly cleansed." When was Goethe cleansed, and how long did he stay out of his wallow?

Another has called attention to a like slip on the part of the same author (Verbum Dei, p. 107). "The unthinking dogma of Orthodoxy that the Bible as such is the Word of God," etc., and later (Verbum Dei, p. 155), "The Bible itself is in so unique and peculiar a sense the Word of God," etc. Be true in statement or else the memory will play you tricks and compel you to contradict yourself.

A third mark of false-scholarship is that it is *purely speculative*. Messrs Driver and Kirkpatrick seek to distinguish between what they call "speculative" and "sober" criticism; but in one place admit that even with "sober" criticism "many of the conclusions are only probable." (p. 9).

The mistake is not a great one; they should have said, "Few of the conclusions are probable." It would seem that the so-called "assured results" of Higher Criticism are not even satisfying their creators. Not long since, Dr. Rade, a leading exponent of this so-called science, declared, "Modern theology is becoming very tired in its researches. * * * We are beginning to see before us certain limitations and checks to our further progress," while Pastor Steinmann, long an ardent advocate of the method, published an article in *"The Christliche Welt"* in which he voices his fears lest the whole structure, reared by the critical scholars, shortly fall to pieces like "a house built of cards." It is significant to say the least, that so great an authority as Prof. Harnack should sicken of his own speculations, and accept the office of librarian, rather than continue his researches after "assured results." All the world knows, how, long since, Prof. Sayce repudiated his own published conclusions, and denounced the whole method as speculative, sinful and soul-destroying. A. J. F. Behrends, one of America's most scholarly pastors, poured out his soul in penitence over having been deceived by this so-called science, and in turn having deceived and misled others. Ah, Paul's injunction to Timothy has occasion still. Let "men turn from the oppositions and babblings of knowledge, falsely so-called."

Finally, listen to Paul's hint, of further obligation as a good minister of Jesus Christ, namely to

DEFEND THE FAITH ONCE DELIVERED.

What is that faith? *The Book itself answers.* Dr. William H. Bates, has recently called attention to the Bible's doctrine of its own inspiration, and has shown that it sets up a claim—clear, strong, unequivocal, to the effect that it is God-given, infallible, inerrant; that its integrity extends to history as well as to morals and religion, and involves expression as well as thought. And for every claim he adduces and even multiplies his texts. (See "Bible Student and Teacher," June, 1906.)

Christ answers that question. No man can read the New Testament and doubt that to Jesus of Nazareth the "faith once delivered" involved the authority and integrity of the Old Testament. He called the Pentateuch "the book of Moses" (Mark 12:26). He read from it, and from the prophets, in the synagogue. (Luke 16:29-31). He reminded His auditors of the obligations involved in Moses' commands. (Matthew 8:4, 19:7-8; Mark 1:44; Luke 5:14).

Alexander Patterson calls attention to the circumstance that Jesus cites from twelve books of the Old Testament and confirms the truth of twenty-four narratives, as follows: Creation, Matt. 19:14; Law of Marriage, Matt. 19:5; Cain and Abel, Matt. 23:25; The Deluge, Matt. 24:37; Abraham, John 8:56; Sodom and Gomorrah, and Lot's wife, Luke 17:28-32; Manna, John 6:49; Brazen Serpent, John 3:14; Shew Bread, Matt. 12:3-4; Elijah and his Miracles, Luke 4:25-26; Naaman, Luke 4:27; Tyre and Sidon, Matt. 11:22; Jonah and "The Whale," Matt. 12:39; The Books of Moses, John 5:46; The Psalms, Luke 20:42; Moses and the Prophets, Luke 24:27; Isaiah, Matt. 13:14; Daniel's prophecies, Matt. 25:15; Malachi, Matt. 11:10. The entire Old Testament, Luke 24:44. Of not one of these does he convey the slightest hint of aught but trustworthiness and literal interpretation. It is noteworthy that Christ has put the seal of his approval upon almost every point disputed by our so-called scholars.

Time also has lent its testimony to the trustworthiness of this "faith." "Of making books there is no end." To make a contribution to literature that shall live is not so easy. P. E. Kipp said truly, "Literature is ephemeral and lasts but a day. Of the three million volumes in the library of Paris, only a few thousand are what may be said to be alive, while the vast numbers are buried in the dust of oblivion, and are mouldy with neglect. But contrary to the universal law, time has but polished the Bible as the ceaseless waves polish the pebbles, and it is today brighter than in all the thirty-five centuries of its existence. It has never been so universally studied, never so widely circulated, and never so generally accepted as now." It is more and more evident that the Master will make His prophecy good, "The heavens and the earth shall pass away, but not one jot or tittle of all that God hath spoken shall fail."

Experience proves the redeeming power of the "faith once delivered." The Bereans "searched the scriptures" and got a blessing. Candace's treasurer read and was redeemed. Peter's auditors listened while he rehearsed what God had spoken, and lived! From that early hour until now not an earnest soul, searching these pages for the way of life, has searched in vain. Only yesterday we looked into the face of Jim Berwick. He is the best-known and most universally loved railroad conductor in America. And yet Jim is not a product of the schools; his learning is extremely limited. He is not a man of large means; his income is a meager one. The secret of his success in life lies in the single circumstance, that some years ago he began to search the pages of Sacred Writ. His first discovery was the discovery of sin. He saw himself as God had long seen him—stained, degraded, undone. He read the sentence of his own doom, "no drunkard shall enter the kingdom of heaven." In an agony of heart he searched on until Jesus, the Lord of Life, loomed before him; and by the printed page He spoke as clearly to Berwick as He ever spake to the blind man at Jericho or to the cripple, carried to His feet, by four; and lo, Jim understood that his "sins were forgiven," and his blindness was removed. He searched on until his justification before God was revealed, until assurance became his sweet experience, until santification was being accomplished in his heart by that same Word. The Scriptures gave birth to his Christian character; by them he is sustaining the same, and out from his life is flowing an influence as holy as was hellish the one which formerly went forth. When he stands before the gathered crowds in colleges and conventions, men forget his defective grammar and seeing that he has been with Christ, seek to be instructed of him. Some days ago, Jim met a man who asked him if he had read Owen, Paine, Hume or Ingersoll? Jim replied in the negative. "Then you are not fit to judge what is right until you have read the other side?" Jim answered him. "You know the kind of a man I was!" "Yes!" "You know what I have been for seventeen years!" "Yes!" "Did you ever hear of the reading of Paine or Ingersoll changing a man like that?" "No!" "Beloved," said Jim, "will you go and read God's Word?"

Chapter II.

THE PROMINENCE OF SKEPTICISM IN OUR SCHOOLS.

"But when some were hardened and disobedient, speaking evil of the way before the multitude, he departed from them and separated the disciples, reasoning daily in the school of one Tyannus. This continued for the space of two years; so that all they that dwelt in Asia heard the word of the Lord, both Jews and Greeks." (Acts 19:8-9). In the previous address we gave consideration to Paul's injunction to Timothy; at this time we call attention to the same apostle at work in a school. He was born to educated parents; he was privileged not alone the best school of his time, but sat at the feet of the greatest instructor of the early centuries—Gamaliel. His accomplishments are evidenced in the office to which he succeeded at an early age; but still more certainly in the literature which he has left us.

The name "Tyrannus" would signify that he stood in the hall of a Greek philosopher, and for two full years reasoned with the crowds who came and went, showing how Old Testament prophecy was fulfilled in the person and work of Jesus Christ. The popularity of his work is argued in the phrase "All they that dwelt in Asia heard the word, both Jews and Greeks." One may easily believe that of the multitudes who heard, a great number must have become converted to the faith that was in Christ.

A school is a good place in which to present the truth. To it, repair youth—always open-minded; or else those more advanced in life, who have retained their anxiety to learn; and the audience is one of special and interesting character on that account. In our day and country the school is one of the most marked features of our civilization; it is everywhere in evidence; and its purpose is supposed to be the impartation and reception of truth.

The old question of Pilate, "What is truth?" can never become obsolete, for the simple reason that all of truth can never be known. The modern conception of a school is not so much that of a bureau of information as it is a room of inquiry; and since skepticism has always bristled with interrogation points, and delighted in assertions, it is natural that it should resort to this center for exploitation.

It will not be disputed that skeptics have chosen the school as

THE SEAT OF DISCUSSION.

To this act no one can urge a valid objection.

The school is appointed for purposes of instruction. The child begins life as empty in mind as nude in body. The old word "education" has lost its original meaning; the school is now supposed to put into the mind what it craves. Dwight Hillis, in his volume, "A Man's Value to Society," says, "The school is to help the boy unpack what intellectual tools he has." That would be a small job. Who can tell what a baby thinks? The school is intended to provide him with intellectual tools, and to train him in the use of them. The child begins life with the tool box empty, but with a craving for knowledge akin to that which the stomach has for food. Men have taken advantage of this, and Tyrannus is only one of the thousands who have opened up places of instruction and have undertaken to provide mental furniture.

The acquisition of knowledge involves investigation. Inquiry is as native as appetite, and by it men have made their progress. Parents are sometimes pestered because children multiply their questions. How else are they to know? If "civilization is a process of self-correction," we can only be corrected by information; and information means investigation. Go into the realm of science, if you please, and you will find that any certitudes are the result of investigation. Hippocrates professed to be a great physician, a medical scientist; but men investigated his claims and discovered his mistakes. Joseph Parker reminds us that when Sir Isaac Newton affirmed that white light consisted of seven different colors it produced a "civil war" among scientists. But investigation demonstrated his claim. Descartes used to be regarded as a kind of idol and to be ranked with Plato and Aristotle and Bacon; but investigation has left "the majority of his speculations to lie in utter ruin." Such instances go to illustrate the Apostle Paul's words, "Whether there be knowledge (or science) it shall pass away." But any science, killed by investigation, were better dead. A nobler one will take its place and the purpose of the school will have found expression in the process. The truth is valuable beyond any man's reputation; and real science is more to be desired than the retention of the most popular theory.

The Scriptures are entitled to no special exemption. Some of us, in boyhood, may have believed that the Bible was so holy a book that to look into its historical veracity, or to question its claims of inspiration were "the unpardonable sin." If so, mature years changed that opinion in favor of an investigation of the very foundation of one's faith that he may know why he believes in the Bible *versus* the Koran; and clings to the Sacred Scriptures as against the Zend Avesta.

There is not an intelligent conservative who has any contention with the student. He may object to the critic, for criticism is commonly a weakness of human nature, and more often imagines the flaws to which it objects than it corrects existing ones. Truly, as a Conservative remarks, "We are not afraid of light. We have no fear of progress; we pray for the expansion and sanctification of scholarship." But we ask for scholarship *versus* speculation; for science *versus* skepticism. Why should lovers of the Bible fear any sort of investigation into the text of their Book—into the question of authorship; into its history; into its prophecy; into its gospels? Is any man so stupid as to suppose that a religion built upon the foundation of falsehood will prove of permanent value to him? To charge Conservatives with such a conception is to reveal ignorance of their character, and indifference to the ordinary civilities of life. Let it be forever understood that when such poets as Milton and

Shakespeare, such philosophers as Bacon and Newton, such statesmen as Bismarck and Gladstone, such reformers as Luther and Wycliff, such scientists as Galileo and Faraday; such preachers as Spurgeon and Parker, such theological professors as Fisher and Broadus, hold the Bible to be *the very Word of God,* they have not done it by closing their eyes to the light and truth, but by being convinced that this Book is the embodiment of both.

No, our objection to the work of "The Higher Critics" is on other grounds altogether; it has to do with the character of their investigation. We charge that they have deliberately introduced intellectual processes which may be properly defined as

A SINISTER METHOD.

Permit us to call attention to four objectionable elements in this method.

1—*The Adoption of a false term.*

"Science' is a good word, and is properly employed when it is applied to the realm of certified knowledge; but when pure speculation is denominated "Science," language suffers and the unthinking are deceived. We do not hesitate to say that this is just the conduct of "The Higher Critics." Their attitude toward the Old Testament; and ever increasingly, their attitude toward the New, is not the attitude of scientific investigation, but of skepticism. What one of them has ever demonstrated by archæology, or history, that the Old Testament characters were mythological, and when did he do it; that the Old Testment history was only "tradition" finding an eventually improved form and literary expression? What one of them has massed his "many infallible proofs" against the deity of Jesus Christ, the record of His miracle-working, His atoning sacrifice, His resurrection from the grave, His ascension to the right hand of God, His ability to make good the promise of return and the establishment of His throne in the earth?

Yet upon all these matters they are in greater or less agreement; but the agreement is an assertion, not a demonstration. Prof. Geo. B. Foster demands, with reference to the bodily resurrection of Jesus Christ, "If it is to be proven, it is to be proven to everyone, the most unbelieving—a scientific pagan for instance." When did these gentlemen present any such proof as that of their critical positions? Who, outside of themselves, have been convinced by their array of arguments, except it be some of the students who have sat at their feet, and whose mental furniture was so scarce that even doubt found greedy reception?

To hear these men exploit the defects of the Bible reminds one of Dr. Jackson's story of the two gentlemen, who, as they were walking down a business street saw an owl perched in the window of a taxidermist. "There," said one, "the man who stuffed that owl did not know what he was about; the feet are not properly placed; the pose of the head is bad; the arrangement of the feathers is unnatural." Just then the owl turned his head and winked; and the self-appointed ornithologist went his way in chagrin. But Higher Critics are not so easily ashamed; ten thousand of their speculations have fallen to the ground before living facts, and yet practically every one of them still calls his vaporings "Science."

2—*The creation of a false forum.*

Critics remind us that since the age is a skeptical one, the school is the proper place for its presentation. They argue "Men and women must meet this attack upon the Scriptures and they may as well do it in their early life," and so men like W. N. Clark, George B. Foster, Prof. H. C. Mitchell, Milton S. Terry, President Bowne, Chancellors Hyde and Day, not to speak of a multitude of others, take the boys at Colgate, Chicago, Boston, Yale, etc., and proceed to champion skepticism in their presence, and array their arguments in favor of its reception, and when the Conservatives complain that such is not the purpose of a theological seminary, the answer is, "These men must meet skepticism; why not in their youth?" The question is not difficult to answer. Youth is not as capable as maturity; the pupil is not supposed to be the equal of the professor; the boy fresh from the farm or the shop—with little knowledge of either science or Scripture—has no fair chance against the man who has practiced polemics for ten, twenty or forty years. It is a world where men have to fight their way, but that would never justify me in putting my children into a roped ring against a Sullivan, to let him bruise their eyes, smash their noses, and knock out their teeth. To call a class-room, where a professor dogmatizes, and students are practically compelled to receive what is said, a "forum of debate" is to juggle with terms with an evil intent. To justify the destruction of the faith in which one was born, and in which his forefathers lived victoriously and died triumphantly, before he becomes capable of deciding whether he should surrender or retain the same, is a piece of robbery beside which the work of highwaymen is a minor incident. To see how such men as these would fare if you pitted them against their equals, and see how soon the suave professor would lose his sweetness, and what appearance he would make when the conflict is over, one needs only to read the controversy which occurred a few years since between Prof. George Burnam Foster and the editor of the Indiana Baptist; or the Chicago daily papers' report of the tilt between Prof. Milton S. Terry and Evangelist W. L. Munhall. Or, if one takes pleasure in a fight between preachers, let him read Dr. Horton's series of "Tentative Suggestions" and Joseph Parker's reply in "None Like It." In every instance he will see illustrated what Parker said in answer to the argument of those who do not receive the conclusions of the skeptics, but who object to their excoriation on the ground "These are nice men and perhaps honest in their convictions." Parker says "I tremble when I am introduced to 'a nice man'; such a 'nice man', such a 'quiet man', such a gentleman.'" You never know what a man is until you have interfered with his vested interests, or until you have seen him under insult. Then you will know how "very nice a man" he is, how "extremely quiet," how absolutely "modest." I have had to do with "nice men" until I dread the term. As James Russell Lowell put it,

"There's a deal of solid kicking
In the meekest looking mule."

All this sweetness of temper about which professors from the Chicago University, once boasted at the mention of Foster's name, faded when the editor of the Indiana Baptist proved more than his match in an argument, and Foster, so far forgot himself as to descend to billingsgate and say at one time, "This is false.'" He also charged the editor with "misrepresentation, defamation, vulgarity and abuse." The whole tone of his expression, in a series of replies, is arrogant and ill-tempered. The halo of the gentleness left the head of Terry when he likened Dr. Munhall to a "cur sitting on his haunches, and barking at the blowing of Gabriel's trumpet."

In a real *forum* these men fare so badly that sweetness is impossible; but in a school-room, where their titles, dominating position and vested powers can compel attention, why should they not be suave for the very sake of seduction?

3—*The adoption of a false philosophy.*

One seldom meets a young graduate from the skeptical theological seminary, but he will find him thanking his stars that he has studied under "higher critical" professors. If he has received their conclusions he is as cock-sure of the results as they are; and if he has rejected them, he is taught to believe that he is all the better for having passed through a period of awful doubts; that his standing ground is all the more sure, because for a while he was without standing ground; that the Bread of Life is all the more palatable by contrast with the poison of which he has tasted. Is such a philosophy sound? Some time since the Larchmont was sunken at sea, and one hundred and seventy people suddenly found themselves struggling in the coldest waves. Seventeen of those were finally saved; 153 of them found a grave in the deep. Shall those seventeen toast their shins at a comfortable hearth and express their gratitude that the Larchmont went down, since, but for its sinking, they never could have appreciated, as perfectly as they ought, the delights of standing upon the solid earth? Such sentiment would sound like the gibberish of the insane; and would express an utter indifference to the fate of the dead. A few years ago, one of the noblest men I ever knew in the flesh, cut from the park what he supposed to be a basket full of mushrooms. His entire family feasted upon them. Four of the five who had partaken finally recovered, but in less than forty-eight hours the noble father was dead. Would our theological professors advise the eating of toad-stools that those who escaped evil results should the more appreciate the real mushroom? And yet, if one had to make a choice between surrendering his friend's body to the poison of the toadstool, or his soul to the deadly effect of unbelief, he would be a false friend indeed who hesitated for one second to choose the former; for is it not written, "Whosoever goeth onward, and abideth not in the teaching of Christ, hath not God."

4—The employment of foul politics.

It is one of the wonders of the present day that skeptical men have so speedily succeeded to so many professorships. The great denominations, an overwhelming majority of whose members believe the Bible from cover to cover, can not understand how it comes about that so many instructors are skeptical. The unsuspecting are told that this is in consequence of the superior education of these men; and that intellectuality and infidelity are now almost synonymous. It is a cute *ruse* but it can not forever remain uncovered. Every man who gets at all close to the denominational machine shortly discovers how these results are secured. There is many a loyal Methodist who goes back from the great annual gathering, sick at heart by reason of the political features of the assembly. The wires that were supposed to be laid underground have protruded, and we have seen them pulled! While they sometimes appear in the candidacy of the bishopric, and more often in connection with appointment to the pastorate, the school office—its presidency and professorship, is where the great *coup* is attempted; and where the skeptical, and of course the "smart men"(?) have succeeded.

In the Baptist denomination, where the church polity is different, the political aspirant is not lacking. The time is now on, when, with that denomination, a successful essential to school appointment seems to be that a man should have expressed his doubt regarding the trustworthiness of the Bible, and so becomes the advanced thinker. This promotion does not occur often enough, and so a Baptist Congress is organized and the honored name of the denomination is compelled to play tail to the kite of Higher Critics. Standing committees for the ordination of men for the ministry, the general adjustment of denominational difficulties, and *sub-rosa*—for the power of pastoral nomination---are eloquently argued in the name of "Progress" and "Advance."

Since the Congregational Church Polity is practically the same, the schemes adopted there follow similar lines; and with kindred results. In the effort to *coup* the whole situation "The Religious Education Association" is formed, and one in ten is a Conservative, chosen to keep up appearances of equity. This association proposes to give us "new (Higher Critic) methods" and "improved (Higher Critic) helps."

Among the Presbyterians of America, wire-pulling by skeptics has not been so successful; and in some notable instances the men who laid hold upon them, found them live wires, and they now lie dead at the place where they accomplished the touch. But it is more and more becoming known that in Scotland, once the very home of this stalwart folk, conservatives have been driven from many professorships, where unpleasant treatment and political wire-pulling methods made such a thing possible, and Prof. James Orr is permitted none too many colleagues "in the faith." Sinister methods are always, and everywhere, open to criticism, but when skeptics adopt them in the name of "scholarship," it is an occasion for such a protest as the great denominations ought now to utter; and by an unequivocal voice, forever end these methods.

But, in conclusion,—

THE SORRY RESULTS.

Time forbids that we should mention more than four of these:

1. *The original purpose of the school is thwarted.* Every school in the land is established in the interest of truth. Even the secular schools are supposed to impart truth—the truth of mathematics, the truth of history, the truth of botany, the truth of geology, the truth of astronomy, and so on. Christian schools, founded and endowed by Christian denominations, are set for all of these, and for the exposition of the Bible addi-

tionally. There are not half a dozen instances in all America, where schools wearing the name of any one of the great denominations, were not founded and fostered by men whose faith in the utter inspiration of the Word was unshaken. What right, then, has infidel teaching within these walls?

It seems bad enough for a University like that of Chicago to be framed on a Baptist foundation, and permit a man to stand in its walls, and deny, in the presence of its theological students, every fundamental of our holy faith, even though it be true that its founder and principal supporter is alive and consents! How much more, when in such an institution as the Northwestern University, baptized in the blood of the saints of the Methodist church, on the occasion of the installation of President James, Prof. Hyde dares to say, "For bishop or minister, or trustee, or pious layman, to interfere with the teachings of a competent university professor on theological grounds, is as wanton and brutal an act as it would be for a prize fighter to step into the pulpit and knock down the minister because he happened to have the bigger fist."

Have we reached the time when a skeptical professor is so important that he can not be asked to answer to the institution that pays his salary, or to the denomination that founds the school? Has the order of the age been inverted, when the servant becomes greater than his lord? Have the ethics of the twentieth century, at the touch of the Higher Critics, taken such a turn that Joseph may now despoil the wife of Pharoah and answer to neither him nor God? If so, the more humble folk have not found it out. God forbid that the secret leak! Only a few days ago a young woman, born and brought up in a non-evangelical home, bred in an atmosphere of ceremonialism, accepted the gospel of regeneration, submitted herself to the ordinace of Bible baptism, and took the consequences of social estrangement. But she had been a teacher in the school of the church which christened her in infancy, and was now urged to continue in the same position! She answered, "You would not want me to teach your children contrary to your faith; and believing as I now do, I could not instruct in accordance with it; and of course it would not be right for me to accept your money for my support while teaching that which you yourselves refuse and reject." She is a plain girl, in a rural district, where the English is poorly spoken; but we insist that her sense of right is the sore need of the so-called "advanced thinkers" of the age; and that if they enjoyed anything akin to it there would be a thousand resignations from American professorships before the breaking of another morn. But a false theology never produced true ethics, and it never can! Perhaps, therefore, we should not complain of these men who jealously guard their salaried positions, while they are about destroying the faith that made them possible; for it is an open secret that not all of them could secure audiences, Ingersoll-like, who would pay $1.00 a head to listen to attacks upon the Word of God. The custom has now become so common as to lose its commercial value. And if these skeptics should resign, how could they maintain their families?

2. *The poor student is speedily despoiled.* We employ the term "poor student" to define on the one side the deleterious effects of infidelity upon his life; and, on the other, to describe his ability. It is a strange fact, yet an incontrovertible one, that the more stupid the man, the more speedily he surrenders to new-fangled notions. Some of the men we knew at the theological seminary are now full-fledged critics; but not one of the full course graduates whose grade was 80 to 100, has succumbed, while several who never did finish it, and never could finish the Seminary's course, have, by a six weeks' course in the Chicago University, made the great discovery that the opening chapters of Genesis are not history, that Abraham was a tribe, Jonah a myth and

Christ a mere man of uncertain ancestry and insecure accomplishments.

There may be another reason for all this! Stupid men—poor students—do not speedily rise in the public estimation, and when such see a man, who for ten years held an unimportant pastorate in their denomination, surrender his faith in the historicity of the Old Testament and his allegiance to the great doctrines of the New, and join himself to a body of so-called liberal thinkers, to be promoted from a salary of $1200 to one of $5,000, and from ministering to 100 people to the pastorate of ten times that number, and from being ignored by his own denomination while he remained with them, to a sudden call to be the University preacher of the denomination, left, it mightily appeals to the little man. This instance is well known. Who knows what the surrender of the faith of one's fathers and of one's Christ may accomplish in the way of promotion? And who can understand what a subtle temptation to the superficial man, is the reputation of being "scholarly?"

On the other hand, when the good student is seduced by the skepticism that wears the mask of scholarship, who can tell what sufferings his believing parents and friends endure; and what pangs may yet take hold upon his very soul? We listened a while ago to an honored father relate the story of having dismissed from his home a noble son, whose faith in the Word of God was unshaken, and whose purpose was the Gospel ministry, to receive back at the end of two years an utter skeptic, who had, as a result of twenty-six lectures on "The Bible as Literature," decided there was no Gospel to preach; and with some pangs of heart, made choice of another profession!

Yet, we ask why so few are entering the ministry? If, perchance, one continues in his ministry, limping his way, until the Lord, from sheer compassion, drops in beside him and unfolds the truth of the Word, as He did to the two on the way to Emmaus, till his holden eyes are open, he may come forth to tell the world, as one has already said of his experience, "Sunday after Sunday I went into my pulpit while my heart was ready to break. I had lost my childhood faith and there was none to take its place. The agony of the 22nd Psalm I knew; but God drew me out of the engulfing waters, out of the pit of miry clay; set my feet upon the rock; established my going, and put a new song into my mouth; . . . and now I know that the Bible is God's Book, and that it is true." But, withal, he will have to weep his way to the grave over the years he has wasted and the undoings he has wrought.

3. *The church is deceived and crippled.* How many of the infected graduates of our skeptical seminaries have dared to tell pulpit committees, corresponding with reference to a call, just what their opinion of the Old Testament was; just what they should say on the subject of "corrupt texts;" "imaginary history," "myth," and what more? When did one of them write to a committee frankly, saying, "If I come to your pulpit, I expect to oppose practically every article your denomination has adopted and to tear to shreds the one relating itself to the inspiration of the Bible?" Why should not these gentlemen be honest? Time and again I have said in my pulpit, and I reaffirm it, that if people do not believe this Book to be God's Word, I do not want them in the membership of my church. How many of our critics dare to take the opposite side, and tell their congregation frankly that if they do believe it, it were better to take their letters and go where such a "fossil faith" is preached?

It is related that Sam Jones used to have a custom of saying to his congregation, "Now, if you don't like what I say, just get up and rack out," and nobody moved. Some fellow, seeing with what pleasantry Sam's congregation received it, thought to adopt it, and he rued the result. They moved almost in a body. Anything like a candid expression of their convictions would empty many of the churches of our Higher Critics. Of course in answer to this, it is said, "One don't need to preach his doubts;" but do our brethren intend to concede, then, that their opinions have reached no firm foundations; that their scholarship is not scientific and positive; that eternal truth is not with them? Hardly; and yet, when one of them remarks, as we have heard a number of them do, "I say these things in this assembly of ministers; I wouldn't care to preach them in my pulpit," he forces us to one of two opinions of him—either he is not convinced of the truth or else he is a coward.

Finally, *Christ is betrayed by His professed friends.* When Judas Iscariot was ready to deliver Him into the hands of His enemies, he turned the trick by a kiss. When the modern critic undertakes the same he accomplishes it by an eloquent speech. In the same book in which Prof. Foster has stripped Christ of His immaculate conception, His infinite wisdom, His sacrificial death, His corporeal resurrection, and His reputed ascension, he has paid Him a multitude of pleasing compliments. But when Judas faced eternity he was filled with a fear that had torment, and no possible search revealed to him a place of repentance. Higher Critics either know Christ or they don't. If they don't know Him, we have the explanation of their inability to receive the Word, "for the natural man receiveth not the things of the Spirit;" if they once knew Him, and were tempted away by this subtle appeal of Satan, "It is written" that "having been enlightened; having tasted of the heavenly gift; having been made partakers of the Holy Spirit; and tasted the good Word of God, and the powers of the age to come, and fallen away, it is impossible to renew them again unto repentance, seeing they crucify to themselves the Son of God afresh, and put Him to an open shame."

My auditors, let me implore you not to follow them into this darkness of unbelief. To me the most terrible description of hell is phrased in the expression "outer darkness." Who can tell what it means to lose the light? A young Baptist minister, making his way by ship to the Holy Land, was visiting in Rome, when word came that smallpox had broken out on board, and the ship was quarantined against his return. What was his dismay a few days later to find himself in that far, strange city, a victim of the dread malady. A native who could speak English was his nurse. Day after day the disease waxed; and his vitality waned. One morning, after a fitful nap, he wakened. His first thought was, "It is night!" Then memory wrought, and he said, "But a few moments ago and the sun was shining into the window," and with anguish that told the story of his alarm, he cried, "Oh, Antonio! Are you there?" And then asked, "Is it day?" Being answered in the affirmative, he cried again, "Oh, Antonio! I am blind! I am blind!" His sight was gone. The next day the struggle was over. He had wakened in the world of Light and walked the streets of the New Jerusalem, where neither sun nor moon are needed, "for the Lamb is the light thereof." But the man who meets the last enemy in "the darkness of unbelief" will be carried down by him into that "outer darkness" of which Jesus spake, the very pall of which is increased by "weeping and wailing and gnashing of teeth." When the blind lead the blind, God pity them both!

Chapter III.

THE PREVALENCE OF SKEPTICISM IN PULPITS.

"Whosoever goeth onward and abideth not in the teaching of Christ, hath not God: he that abideth in the teaching, the same hath both the Father and the Son. If any one cometh unto you, and bringeth not this teaching, receive him not into your house, and give him no greeting: for he that giveth him greeting partaketh in his evil works." (2 John 9-11). This text is chosen as the starting point for this discourse, not because it involves disfellowship, but because it describes, with accuracy, the conduct and opinions of some who now occupy evangelical pulpits. If one could exercise his own preference in the discussion of such a theme as this, he would yield to the temptation of kindly speech at the expense of truth, and of compromise at the cost of candor. There is no more painful experience than that of being compelled to impeach either the motive or the conclusions of the fellows of one's own profession. And yet there are times in which one must make choice between surrendering the very name of his calling, or else disfellowship those who have trailed its nobility in the dust.

In the profession of Bible teaching that time is now on, and the Scripture selected for consideration plainly indicates the conduct which must characterize him who remains loyal to "the teachings of the Christ." The text describes the progressive pastor, indicates the point of separation, and demands the end of fraternity.

THE "PROGRESSIVE" PASTOR.

"Whosoever goeth onward and abideth not in the teaching of Christ." It is a significant fact that the very phrase "goeth onward" (*proagon*) is practically identical with our word "progressive" which has been voluntarily assumed by the Bible critics of our times.

In discussing those of them who are pastors, we propose to follow the plan adopted in dealing with the scholars—namely, to employ the names of three or four pastors whose wide-spread reputation, lofty position, and theological opinions make them easily leaders among so-called liberal pastors, and invite your consideration to their recent utterances. Perhaps none will object if the names of Dr. Fischer, pastor at Berlin, Germany; Dr. R. J. Campbell, successor to Joseph Parker, London, England; Dr. Crapsey, recently removed from the Episcopal pastorate, and Dr.

Lyman Abbott—the best known Congregationalist in America, are chosen. I should be very glad indeed, being a Baptist, to name a notable man of my own denomination; but while we are honeycombed with Higher Criticism, the denomination has no pastor, either in the old or new world, holding to higher critical views and at the same time occupying a specially exalted pulpit.

In studying the utterances of the above named, and even of scores of others who are their confederates in opinion, we find agreement at three points, which goes to make up the claim of the progressive pastor.

1. *He knows his methods to be scientific:* Dr. Fischer, before the Convention of the Protestant Verein reminded his auditors of that fact in the following way: "There can no longer be any claim to a revelation in the old sense of the word. The idea is not in agreement with the *certain results of modern scientific research.* It is beyond doubt that the investigations of science and history, and the unprejudiced researches into the character of original Christianity, which have been going on for about seventy years without regard to dogmas and doctrines, have made religion something entirely different from what it had traditionally been supposed to be, etc." His defenders also demanded the full liberty of theological expression in the name of "scientific in-

dependence" and inveighed against the abridging of "freedom of expressing theological views in the churches" and of the "independence of *scientific* investigators."

Dr. Campbell, in his very recent declaration concerning what he calls "Restated Theology," reminds the public that "The new theology, in common with the whole scientific world, believes that the finite universe is one aspect or expression of God, but it thinks of 'It' or 'Him' as consciousness rather than a blind force, thereby differing from some scientists." Dr. Crapsey, in his defense of the denial of the Immaculate Conception, said that this interpretation has been forced upon him by a "knowledge of the facts."

Americans are well enough acquainted with Lyman Abbott's positions to know that he holds them all to be "scientific."

Profession is one thing; possession is another. It is not certain that there is a scientist in the views quoted. The Consistory of Berlin, composed of the ecclesiastical superiors of Dr. Fischer, in calling upon him to resign his office on account of preaching contrary to the doctrines of the church, said, "His views are those of a man who is not yet mature in his theological thinking."

If any one ever suspected R. J. Campbell of being "scientific" we have yet to learn his name. Even Canon Henson, himself a radical higher critic, when asked whether Campbell's liberal movement in London would amount to anything, is reputed to have replied, "No, I think it is a tempest in a teacup,; I do not think the element of a movement is in it at all."

As for Dr. Crapsey, if he had discovered "facts" which disproved the immaculate conception, he should have marshalled them before his judges and so saved both himself and his mistaken denomination.

Dr. Abbott's science is not that of an investigator; but that of an orator, whose facts are commonly eloquently phrased fancies.

It is possible, therefore, that these gentlemen, in common with the great company who call themselves "scientific," profess that which they do not possess. It does not make a profession scientific to name it so. An old colored woman in the South was addressed by one of our great statesmen, who happened to be riding by her cabin, "Auntie, are those your boys?" She replied, "Dey is not my chillen; dey is my grandchillen." "What are their names?" "Well, dem chillen has right smaht names; dis one is named de Apossle Paul; and dat one is named de Epissle Petah." But the name did not make an apostle of the first; nor an epistle of the second. We would like some gentleman who is truly scientific to pass judgment upon Campbell's statement. "The whole scientific world believes that the finite universe is one aspect or expression of God, but it thinks of It or Him as consciousness rather than a blind force, thereby differing from some scientists." Who are the scientists that do not belong with "the whole scientific world?" Positively a speech like that reminds one of nothing so much as the introductory remark of a colored man in Texas on the occasion of Thanksgiving day: "My bredren, dis am de day when de gov'ment of dis United States calls upon de hole civilized wurld to present itself a livin' sacrifice to demonstrate de administration."

I do not say that the man who claims that his theology is in line with "the whole scientific world" is *non compos mentis;* he may yet have some notions that are intelligent; but in all likelihood they are few enough to warrant the fumigation of his opinions on the principle that was involved in the report of "The Baltimore American." A man said, "Why did they insist on fumigating that poor old bookworm's manuscripts?" to which his friend replied, "I suppose they were afraid it might contain some germs of thought."

2. *He speaks the shibboleth of skepticism.* Henry Van Dyke, speaking of this age of doubt, says, "Its coat of arms is an interrogation point rampant, above three bishops dormant, and its motto is Query?" Later he argues that science

has been corralled in the name of skepticism and made to appear hostile to religion? In literature "skepticism in all its shades and degrees, from the most clear, self-conscious and aggressive, to the most vague, diffused, and deprecatory, is reflected in the current productions. He traces it in the lay sermons of Huxley, Tyndall, Harrison and Clifford. He names these men "Knight-errants of Doubting Castle." He affirms that skepticism hangs like a cloud over the fragmentary but majestic life-philosophies of Carlyle and Emerson. He remarks, truly, "in the vivid and picturesque historical studies of Renan and Froude, skepticism is at once ironical and idealistic, destructive and dogmatic." He says, "In the novels of unflinching and unblushing naturalism, like those of Zola and Maupassant, and the later works of Thomas Hardy, skepticism speaks with a harsh and menacing accent of the emptiness of all life and the futility of all endeavor." "In many of the later novels of the day we find no recognition, even between the lines, of the influence which the idea of God or its absence, the practice of prayer or its neglect, actually exercises upon the character and conduct of men." He affirms that even poetry has fallen under the spell: "we hear today the voice of skepticism most clearly 'making abundant music around an elementary nihilism, now stripped naked.'"

How natural that men should inhale what is in the atmosphere, and ministers are only men. There was a time when the preacher's only temptation was to carnality. His confidence in a personal God, in an inspired Book, in a sin-bearing Saviour was not only unshaken, it was undisturbed. The times were slow and it was not difficult for him to be always abreast of them; now they are steaming and flashing like lightning and he is told he must keep abreast still, and the times are skeptical. "If I hold to 'the faith once delivered' how can I deal with an age which has denied it? How can I gain audience with men who have pushed past the position I occupy? How can I command the respect, and accomplish the conversion of those who subscribe to the latest scientific magazine, unless I speak their shibboleth, and let them know that I still stand at their side?" This is the subtle temptation! Men, and even ministers forget that the way to turn back the galloping herd, is not to take their course and keep up with them, but to take a stand and call after them. The skeptical preacher can no more assist the skeptical sinner than a drowning man can assist his sinking friend. Christ was not speaking of a journey in unbelief when he said, "Whosoever shall compel thee to go with him one mile, go with him twain."

All through the Northland of the United

States, our so-called "sacred press" teems with articles written by advanced thinkers who are telling us how up-to-date theology is essential to success in dealing with the keen, well-trained intellects of the hour. But the reports made at every annual gathering, of men, women and children won even to their churches, not to say to Christ, belie their boast. A more ineffectual gospel has never been preached than that which Mr. Campbell names "The New Theology;" and as for its advocates in the pulpit, it is a notorious fact that if Conservatives did not visit their churches once a year to hold a series of meetings they would face the shame of utter failure in reaching men. The only point of profit, therefore, in this whole position, seems to be that which Victor Hugo sums up when speaking of Tholomeys, the rich old roue, who had "replaced his teeth by jests, and his hair by joy, and his health by irony, and made verses now and then on any subject." "However," said Hugo, "he doubted everything with an air of superiority—a great power in the eyes of the weak."

3. *To the progressive pastor the faith of the fathers is fogyism.* There is not one of these pastors but has at some time spoken of the convictions of the Conservatives as "the traditional view." When the great Gladstone was alive and writing his book "The Impregnable Rock of

Holy Scripture" he spoke of Prof. Huxley's description of the battle of Faith in which Huxley speaks of "the old fashioned artillery" of the churches on the one side and the "weapons of precision" used by the advancing forces of science on the other. Think, will you, of Joseph Parker, in London, England, battling away with nothing better than the "old-fashioned artillery" of the churches—"The Gospel" of which Paul was "not ashamed;" while his successor in office, R. J. Campbell, comes to the conflict with the "weapons of precision"—the development of Modern Science. And yet, somehow or other, Parker accomplished things,—constructed a great building; called together a great congregation, produced great books, and better yet, aided in the great development of hundreds and thousands of lives. Now his successor, R. J. Campbell, with the "weapons of precision—the development of modern science" is destroying a congregation, weakening the faith of his fellows, starting on a campaign in the interests of "restated theology" that his confrere in skepticism, Canon Henson, calls, "a storm in a teacup, with no element of a movement in it."

Joseph Parker proudly confesses his allegiance to "the faith once delivered;" "the faith of the fathers;" the faith that presents "a personal God;" "an infallible Book," "a Divine Christ," "a salvation from sin through His sufferings." There are "dogmas" in that faith; but dogma does not necessarily oppose science; it may express it. There is nothing in all the universe so uncompromising, so dogmatic as science—which is also God's revelation. Conservatives do not hold their dogmas simply because they have been stated and their fathers have held them true; they believe them on scientific grounds. "The heavens declare the glory of God and the firmament showeth his handiwork." It is the work of a person, not of a "force;" of intelligence, not of "fortuitous circumstances." They believe the Bible to be inspired because there is every evidence of it! The historical evidence is conclusive! It is far more reasonable to suppose that the nations round about Israel borrowed from Israel's faith and corrupted what they borrowed, than it is to believe that Israel borrowed from the nations round about and completed what she borrowed. It may not be in keeping with the exploded theory of evolution, but it is in perfect accord with the facts of history that men more often and more easily build up a false faith than they construct a true one. We believe that Christ was the Son of God because it does not offend our reason. There is nothing unreasonable in the idea that God should beget, in the flesh—One like unto Himself—and give His Son to the world as the Saviour from its sins. To deny that is to deny the central truth of all theology—old or new—namely, "God is Love." "Greater love hath no man than this, that a man lay down his life for his friends, but God commended his love toward us in that while we were yet sinners Christ died for us." The Bible plan of salvation appeals to Reason.

We believe that His death was an atonement for sin partly because it is according to Revelation; but particularly because it is according to Reason. All that we know in this life confirms that claim. There is no sin that is ever atoned for without the suffering of somebody—and quite often the innocent have to suffer for the guilty. Call it dogmatic if you like; name its advocates "back-numbers," speak of them as "old fogies" and all that; but do not forget that up to this present time, with all your boasted progress, you cannot present a point of improvement upon the old theory and the old Book. What have you added to its moral code? What satisfactory substitute have you given for the old doctrine of inspiration? What have you permanently subtracted from it to make it more trustworthy? The world is waiting for a better theory of creation than Genesis 1:1—"In the beginning God created the heaven and the earth;" for a better plan of salvation than John 3:16—"God so loved the world that he gave his only begotten son, that whosoever believeth in him should not perish, but have everlasting life;" for a more satisfactory expression of inspiration than Hebrews 1:1—"God, who at sundry times and in divers manners, spake in time past unto the fathers by the prophets, hath in the end of these days spoken unto us in His Son."

THE POINT OF SEPARATION.

"If any one cometh unto you and bringeth not this teaching receive him not into your house and give him no greeting."

There can be no controversy concerning the meaning of this passage. To accept it at what it says necessitates separation from those who deny "the teachings of Christ." It is plainly affirmed "They have not God."

But this involves other questions.—

How do we know what Christ taught? What are the sources of information? Conservatives say, "the Gospels; the Book of the Acts, and some of the epistles." Here we have the purported report of the teachings of Christ by eye-witnesses. They report Christ as having been begotten by the Holy Spirit, in keeping with prophecy. (Matt. 1:20, 23). They report Christ as having claimed equality with the Father, "I and my father are one." They report Christ as having willingly laid down His own life, "I lay down my life; no man taketh it from me." They report Christ as having taught that salvation depended upon one's faith in Him, "No man cometh unto the Father but by me." They report Christ as having risen from the dead, and record many of His post-resurrection teachings. They report Christ as having ascended up to the right hand of God; and record what He said in the very act of ascent.

Now our progressive pastors are almost at one in insisting that "the Gospels are full of errors, and demand in various parts very unequal credence." Mr. W. H. Mallock says "They speak of Christ's spoken discourses as 'often nothing more than vague conjectures of the evangelists.'" They describe them as "subjective visions," "unwarranted imaginations," etc. Perhaps these Progressives will permit a question? "How do they know these things?" Conservatives have the testimony of eye-witnesses concerning the teachings of Jesus. No intelligent man will claim that the canon of the New Testament is essentially changed from what it was when first it came from the hands of its authors. And it is by the writings of these men that our Christ lives in our faith. Who created the Christ "Progressives" describe? What witnesses have they as to who He was and what He taught? Is it possible that critics in the pastorate have accomplished what critics in the schools say is an impossibility? Have we not already read from Dr. Driver, "It is ridiculous to imagine that history can be rewritten by a series of unsupported guesses, however ingenious." What scientific support have these gentlemen for their guesses? R. F. Horton tells us that in the ruined abbey of St. Albans the restorers found unnumbered fragments of painted stone trodden into the ground behind the chancel. "When these were collected and carefully placed together the shrine of the saint was recovered, which stands now in its completeness, a visible proof that the fragments had originally belonged to the whole. In the same way we are able to take the scattered utterances, the thoughts of Jesus, and fit them together until a lovely and harmonious structure of doctrine arises before our eyes."

But whence are we to find them? The Conservatives bring the material for the image of their Christ from Matthew, Mark, Luke, John, and Acts. The Progressives have repudiated these as non-dependable. Who is providing them with the material which they are piecing together? Matthew we know, Luke we know, Mark we know, John we know, Paul we know; but who are these that are providing material out of which the Christ of "new theology" is being created?

Our policy is expressed in Scripture thus: "Search the scriptures for they are they that testify of me." Let Progressives tell us whence they bring their testimony, seeing that they have already discarded what prophet and apostle have said.

Who refuses to abide in Christ's teachings? The man who denies that God is the Father of Christ, for Christ claimed it; the man who denies that Christ is the equal of God, for Christ claimed that; the man who denies that Christ died for sinners, Christ affirmed it; the man who denies that Christ was raised on the third day, Christ predicted it, and afterward proclaimed its fulfillment; the man who denies that Christ ascended bodily into the heavens, Christ promised it and in the presence of above five hundred witnesses accomplished it; the man who denies that Christ is coming again with His holy angels to reign in the earth, it is Christ's repeated assertion. There is not a one of these doctrines that higher critical pastors have not opposed and even excoriated. Fischer did it in Berlin; Campbell has just accomplished it in London. He affirms that Christ is no more divine than we are; he affirms that man is not a sinner, but an increasing conquerer, saying, "The fall of man in a literal sense is untrue." "The doctrine of sin which holds us to be blameable for deeds that we cannot help, we believe to be a false view." Again, "We reject wholly the common interpretation of the atonement, that another is beaten for our fault." "We believe not in the final judgment, but in the judgment that is ever progressing, etc."

Dr. Bettex, one of Germany's greatest scholars, in his book, "The Bible—the Word of God," sums up the views of "Progressives," after this manner, "According to this radical criticism is there any inspiration? None! Any Trinity? None! Any fall into sin? None! Any devil or angel? None! Any miracles? None. Any law from Mount Sinai? None! Any wrath of God! No! Is the death of Christ vicarious? No! Did Christ rise from the dead? No! Has there been any outpouring of the Holy Ghost? No! Will there be any resurrection of all the dead, or a final judgment? No."

But even all of this is not the end. Dr. Lyman Abbott, not many months since, before one of our greatest universities, defined God as "A Force." Dr. Campbell says "The new theology thinks of IT or HIM as consciousness." Here is a point, at least, in which they approach "science" but it is the "science" of Mrs. Eddy, who asks the question, "is God a person?" and answers it, "No! God is not a person; God is a principle."

It would seem as if we are not far from the day when ministers of the Gospel will have to do as Dr. A. C. Dixon did in a convention of free-thinkers in New York City. An up-to-date theologian, in the person of a lawyer, had made an eloquent address, one sentence of which was "I worship the everlasting IT." When Dixon came to deliver himself on "The Simplicity of the Gospel" he said, "Brethren, if many of you are at the shrine of the former speaker, let me utter a word of warning; people grow like the thing they worship, and the first thing you know this town will be full of 'ITS'."

What shall the believing do about it? Dr. Stocker, former court preacher of Berlin, says, in answer to this question, "The critic's denial of practically all that conservative believers regard as the very foundation of Christianity, such as the divine inspiration of the scriptures, the Trinity, the atonement, and the divinity of Christ, virtually puts them outside the pale of the historical, evangelical church. There is no common ground between the old and the new schools of theology. It is time to decide what ought to be done in the matter. Evidently the best course would be to separate peacefully the liberals from the protestant churches. Let them go out and organize and maintain congregations after their own manner and creed. Some of the churches and parishes may be left in their hands as honesty and justice demand; but let them remain no longer in the church whose faith they do not share. They represent no type of Protestant Christianity. They are the teachers of a new religion." This would seem to be the only course open that retains the semblance of ethical conduct. "Can two walk together except they be agreed?" Dr. P. S. Henson says, "between these two schools there is the width of the whole heaven;" and Dr. A. H. Strong says, "we seem to be on the verge of another unitarian defection." Why should we not part in peace?

And yet, in answer to this kindly proposition, Dr. Rade, says, "We moderns will risk anything rather than leave the Church." It looks a little like the old story of the drunken man who had made his way homeward to the point of the lamp-post, to which he affectionately clung, saying, "together we stand; divided I fall." And yet sad as is that prospect, Conservatives must even insist upon it; or else play truant to the text, "If any come unto you and bringeth not this teaching, receive him not into your house and give him no greeting, for he that giveth him greeting partaketh in his evil works."

THE END OF FRATERNITY.

Christian fraternity is not merely social. If it were, Conservatives and Critics could adjust their differences, or even afford to forget and neglect them. I have no creed to which my neighbors must subscribe in order to be loved as neighbors; no doctrinal standards to which my acquaintances must come before I call them friends. That is another matter altogether! Among the Unitarians I have some close personal friends; and so among Universalists, and so with Christian Scientists and Dowieites! But our fellowship is social; it is not a fellowship of faith. The question of Christian fraternity is not necessarily involved.

Christian fraternity is not even ecclesiastical. It is well known that men may be members of the same church and not be special friends; in fact in our larger churches they are not even speaking acquaintances in all instances. Every great denomination has its thousands, and even its millions of members upon whose faces the most widely traveled brother of that faith has never looked. And, of the few he does know, there may be some who belong to a local body of believers with him, and yet with whom he refuses to fraternize. So Christian fraternity is not a question of ecclesiastical relations.

Fraternity "in Christ" involves "the fellowship of a common faith." Mark you, "The fellowship of a common faith." Two people may consent to the same creed and yet hate each other—they are without the "fellowship" of a common faith. Two men may love each other, the one be a Unitarian and the other an Evangelical; they also are without the fellowship of "a common faith;" and their fraternity is not the fraternity "in Christ."

When Charles Spurgeon quit the Baptist Union of England he did not do it because he hated all the brethren of the Union, but because he found many of them accepting and preaching "another faith" than that revealed in God's Word. The man who criticises Spurgeon's conduct ought also to complain of John's injunction as voiced in this text. Truly, as one has said, "It is not for us to become judges of motive; or to defame men simply because they differ from us. Neither is it for us to contradict the inspired record of the Word of God when it declares that 'certain men became vain in their imaginations and their foolish heart was darkened' and 'they changed the truth of God into a lie, and worshipped and served the creature more than the Creator, who is blessed forever.'"

Paul, writing to Timothy, warned him against those "men who, concerning the truth have erred, saying that the resurrection is passed already," and "overthrown the faith of some." Peter affirmed there will be "false prophets bringing in privily destructive heresies, denying even the Master that bought them . . . . by reason of whom the way of truth shall be evil spoken of." John, in his first epistle said, "Who is the liar but he that denieth that Jesus is Christ? Whosoever denieth the Son the same hath not the Father." In his Second Epistle, he calls upon us to reject the fellowship of all such. (V. 9-10.)

The day in which evangelical Christianity so far compromises with critics that He who stilled the tempest by the word of his power, who fed the thousands with five loaves of bread, who healed the nobleman's son, who raised Jarius' daughter from the dead, who restored the deaf, the blind, the dumb by a word, who cleansed the leper by a look, is no longer enthroned in our faith as the Messiah of the prophets—the Son of God, the Saviour from sin—the light that has shone for millenniums upon the paths of men is extinguished and the world is doomed. But surrender we will not! Our Saviour is too precious to be betrayed into the hands of His enemies; the Word of God is too glorious to be flung away at the behest of blind leaders; our message from heaven is too sweet to our sin-sick souls for us either to reject the messengers or to doubt the truth they delivered once for all.

Chapter IV.

THE THEORY OF EVOLUTION AND FALSE THEOLOGY.

"In the beginning God created the heavens and the earth . . . . And God, said, Let the waters under the heavens be gathered together unto one place, and let the dry land appear: and it was so. . . . . And God said, Let the earth put forth grass, herbs yielding seed, and fruit-trees bearing fruit after their kind, wherein is the seed thereof, upon the earth: and it was so. . . . . And God said, Let the waters swarm with swarms of living creatures, and let birds fly above the earth in the open firmament of heaven. And God created the great sea-monsters, and every living creature that moveth, wherewith the waters swarmed, after their kind, and every winged bird after its kind; and God saw that it was good. . . . . And God said, Let the earth bring forth living creatures after their kind, cattle, and creeping things, and beasts of the earth after their kind: and it was so. . . . . And God said, Let us make man in our image, after our likeness: and let them have the dominion over the fish of the sea, and over the birds of the heavens, and over the cattle, and over all the earth, and over every creeping thing that creepeth upon the earth. And God created man in his own image, in the image of God created he him; male and female created he them." Gen. 1:1, 9, 11, 20-21, 24, 26-27.

"By faith we understand that the worlds have been framed by the word of God, so that what is seen hath not been made out of things which appear." Heb. 11:3.

Our theme is "The Theory of Evolution and False Theology." It may not have occurred to all that the theory of evolution and false theology are indissolubly linked together. But every scientist understands, as do also intelligent teachers of the Scriptures, that the theory of evolution is not simply a question of the origin of species; but, in its present-day application, proposes to account for everything material, from fire-mist to the perfected frame of the universe; everything animated, from the sterilized cell of lowest life to the Man of Nazareth; and everything moral, from the sensations of an amoeba to the sacred communion between God and man.

When, therefore, a biologist says that the minister has nothing to do with the theory of evolution, he reveals either his ignorance of its application, or his indisposition to be disturbed by an adequate argument. When a professor in Natural Science says that people who are not constant students of his specialty should not pass any judgment upon its claims and contentions, he disputes the right of decision by a competent jury, and demands that the public close its eyes, that it may the more readily swallow his deliverances.

It may be necessary, therefore, for the man who decides to think for himself, and even maintain his right to judge the findings of so-called scientists, to "beg pardon;" but this formality performed, we pass on to question, compare, and conclude according to the individual judgment.

Every preacher of the present hour is compelled to deal with the theory of evolution, and either accept it or reject it. Its advocates have invaded his realm. Prof. Metcalf, biologist of the Woman's College, Baltimore, in his book "Organic Evolution" naively tells us that in coming to the position of a dignified science the last stronghold to be taken by evolution was that of the supernaturalist, "that of the man who claims that supernatural agency intervenes in nature in such a way as to modify the natural law of events." This opinion he thinks Darwin overthrew and doomed. (See "Introduction to Organic Evolution" p. 20).

Such a suggestion simply indicates that the entire company of conservative theologians are not only unscientific, but are mental mossbacks, clinging to exploded theories, preaching obsolete opinions, and practicing doctrine long since out of date. If, therefore, one of them should fail to make an argument, the public ought not to be surprised. On the other hand, if he should succeed in making the theory of evolution look doubtful, it might be worth while for the public to examine carefully the foundations of this much boasted philosophy.

At the risk of revealing our weakness in argument, we propose three statements concerning evolution. First, The Theory is Unscientific; second, The Theory is Unscriptural; third, The Theory is Anti-Christian.

THE THEORY IS UNSCIENTIFIC.

It is a suggestion, not a science. The prevailing opinion that evolution is a modern scientific discovery is false alike to history and to the proper employment of speech. On the authority of Wallace, Lucretius, who lived a hundred years before Christ, in his great poem on "The Nature of Things" expressed the major part of the present-day theory. He held to the molecular belief, that the molecules did not come into actual contact; defined atoms, thought that they were eternal; while admitting the existence of gods, he refused them any share in the construction of the universe, maintaining that it had come by chance, after infinite time, by random motions and collisions, and he tried to account for the introduction of sensation into atoms. He maintained that earth worms came by spontaneous generation, and that in some remote period of the world's history, when heat and moisture abounded, the earth was filled with wombs, out of which were born living things, and after the custom of many a present-day biologist he contended that the very ground had given existence alike to the lowest forms of life, to every beast and to man.

To be sure, the modern apostles of this faith—Huxley, Darwin, Spencer, Wallace and others, have found for it more attractive phrases; argued it on the ground of likelihood, progression and analogy; but not one of these ever called it a science. They regarded it a theory, and a theory only. It is not unusual for the smaller followers of great minds to far exceed their masters. The leading evolutionists of the world today do not speak of it as a "science;" they retain the old term of Huxley, Darwin, and Spencer—"theory." But many a preacher who is neither a specialist in natural history nor in supernatural revelation, finds himself involved in what he regards "the conflict between science and theology" and attempts the reconciliation. Since the path by which Science has traveled is strewn with the decaying structures of discarded theories, why should not Andrew White withhold his endeavor until specialists in biology, geology and paleontology are themselves convinced that evolution is something more than a theory?

Several times in recent years we have questioned fairly competent exponents of this theory as to whether they regarded it a "science," to be answered in almost every instance, "Well, it is generally adopted, the world over, as a working theory for scientific investigation." Now the Standard Dictionary defines "theory" after this manner—"A plan, or scheme subsisting in the mind, but based on principles variable by observation; loosely and popularly, mere hypothesis or speculation; hence an individual view." "Science," on the contrary, it describes as "Knowledge gained and verified by exact observation and correct thinking." A theory may be scientific; but to make it such one must produce its verification by exact observation or experiment, whereupon it is no longer a theory. Neither Huxley, Darwin nor Spencer ever maintained that they had produced such verification of evolution!

But we go a step farther. *The theory of evolution is unproven and unprovable.* Notwithstanding Darwin's "Origin of Species," in the form of a book, the occurrence of a new species, either by natural selection or human cultivation, is unknown. By cultivation man has made the rose more splendid in size, more beautiful and variegated in color, and not a few of the flowers he has even doubled; but no man has yet produced a rose from the seed of sunflower, nor from the pink, nor from anything else than a rose; or even been able to make a grain of rye, similar as it is to the form of other cereals, bring forth oats or wheat, or else than rye. A line from Genesis is the law of natural history. "Every seed after its own kind." The scientists of the world were never so anxious, upon any single point, and never wrought so assiduously to disprove it, as they are to do away with this statement of Holy Scripture; but their endeavors to overthrow the Divine fiat have signally failed.

When a biologist who believes that all life, from an amoeba to a Milton, is the product of evolution, being asked if such a thing as a new species by natural selection is known, answers, "We think there are some snails in the Hawaiian Islands that hint at it," he will not blame us if we regard his investigations a little "slow." Or, if he affirms that the gill slits of a human foetus prove that man has ascended from sea life, we answer, "That sounds fishy." If he point to the mule in defense of his doctrines, we remind him of its sterility, and make his argument asinine. Not a few scientists have said, concerning the mule, that with his accustomed stubbornness he "blocks the way of the evolution theory." But better still is the remark of Dr. A. J. Frost that "the mule is the endeavor of an ass to evolute himself, but he only succeeds in making a bigger ass of himself."

The utter desperation to which evolutionists are driven in their desire to "demonstrate"—as the Christian Scientist says—and so be able to switch from theory to science, is shown in their treatment of the horse. They have dug out of the earth a little animal about the size of a fox, with five toes, which has some similarity to the horse, and they have called him—old horse—eohippus; and they have brought up another with three toes, as big as a timber wolf, and because of certain similarities they have called him a horse; and then they have imagined that horse finally developing into the present beautiful beast of domestic service, with one toe elongated from the knee to the hoof; and in certain splints on the side of his leg they find the aborted ties. The intervening horses, bridging the gap between these ancient animals and our black beauty, they have sought in vain! Yet they will stand before you and speak with all the assurance of men who had found the last missing link, concerning the evolution of the horse! Why do they begin with that little fox-like animal? In the ocean there is a shrimp that has the head of a horse and his motions in water are much like a plunging charger. Why not begin with him? At college the boys used to be chargeable with having ridden a pony, and if it could be proven it was worse for them when they came into the professor's presence. Once a cute lad, who was later a consul in one of the South American Republics, bluntly remarked in the presence of our professor, "I had a pony last season that thirteen rode, but I gave him away because this present class has nineteen big fellows in it, and I thought it would be an outrage for us all to straddle the little fellow!" But that poor pony of the five toes has been straddled by a thousand professors; they have ridden the toes off him, and it is little wonder that some of their students have gone out to pity the pony and regard the professors' conduct with ridicule.

Something similar has occurred in the attempt to make a man out of a monkey. They found the missing link once in "The Calaveras Skull." It was 150 feet below surface. There could be no doubt about it! But when Wm. R. C. Scribner confessed that he had brought it into tne mine as a practical joke, scientists were ashamed. Dr. W. J. Sinclair's discussion, "Recent Investigations Bearing on the Question of the Occurrence of Neocene Man in the Auriferous Gravels of the Sierra Nevada" confirms Scribner's claim, and makes it perfectly evident that Prof. J. D. Whitney paraded a very modern skull as that of a prehistoric man.

They found the missing link in the Neanderthal skeleton in Prussia, and proclaimed it three hundred thousand years old; but it turned out to be only a Cossack killed in 1814. Columbia College had a smart professor who dug out of Colorado's soil a skeleton. It was heralded as of remarkable antiquity, and the friable bones were being paraded to the ends of the earth when some cowboys complained that the grave of their pet monkey had been rifled. I was taken into a little pavilion near Manitou and was shown the petrified (?) body of a remarkable little fat fellow who had been brought up from the bottom of the Colorado River. But a man needed not to be a scientist, to discover that it was nothing more than a figure hewn out of stone. To be sure, the greatest ado has been made over the Pithecanthropus Erectus. It consists of the piece of a skull and leg bone and two teeth, found in Java, in 1891. Dr. Alexander Patterson says, the cubic measurement of that skull is sixty inches—the same as that of an idiot. These specimens were found at separate places and times. The skull is too small for the thigh bone. The age of the strata in which they were found is uncertain. Even Haeckel admits that the belief that this is the missing link is strongly combated by some distinguished scientists.

The earth has been opened at a thousand points; the sea has been explored to its bottom; biologists have had access to the very bowels of both and have been animated by one determination—the discovery of the missing link—and yet to the present hour they have utterly failed to produce it! We fear that it is an illustration of what the Irishman said. He attended the circus and was especially interested in the animals. When they brought out the dromedary he examined the ungainly beast from head to foot; felt of the great humps to see whether they were artificial or actual flesh. Being convinced of the latter, he said, "Begory; they ain't no sich animal!" This seems to be the truth concerning the missing link. It is one thing to imagine that it exists; it is another to make the demonstrations, and science demands the latter.

Its conclusions are without premises. What evidence is there that the universe began in fire mist? What evidence is there that life originated out of death? What evidence is there that mineral became the vegetable, and vegetable became the animal, and the animal became the man?

What proof have we of the eternity of matter beyond the atheistic desire to have it so? And, if these premises are false how can conclusions resting upon them be true? If within the knowledge of man the reptile has never become a bird, a fish has never become a mammal, a monkey has never become a man; if the depths of the earth and the sounding of the seas refuse to deliver up a single instance of such a metamorphosis, what are the premises of this argument? It may be very convenient to push your claims back to the time where the knowledge of man utterly fails, but do not do violence to the splendid attainments of human speech by calling such conduct "scientific." I may have no right to object to Mr. Darwin's believing that "man is descended from a hairy quadruped, furnished with a tail, and pointed ears; probably arboreal in its habits, and an inhabitant of the Old World," but I can not be denied the right to ask him to produce some evidence of his assertion. Dr. Eldridge, of the British Museum, declares that that institution is filled with specimens, every one of which disproves the evolution theory. Dr. Joseph Clark, after spending twenty-nine years in the heart of Africa, says: "I find no evidence of evolution in Africa, but positive proofs to the contrary."

THE THEORY IS UNSCRIPTURAL.

The Word nowhere warrants it. There are brethren in the pulpit who have a new way of interpreting the first chapter of Genesis, which, by the way, one of my fellow-laborers has translated after the following manner:

1. Primarily the unknowable moved upon cosmos and evolved protoplasm.

2. And, protoplasm was inorganic and undifferentiated; containing all things in potential energy; and a spirit of evolution moved upon the fluid mass.

3. And the Unknowable said, Let atoms attract; and their contact begat light, heat and electricity.

4. And the Unconditioned differentiated the atoms each after its kind; and their combination begat rock, air and water.

5. And there went out a spirit of Evolution from the Unconditioned, and working in protoplasm by accretion and absorption produced the organic cell.

6. And cell by nutrition evolved primordial germ, and germ developed protogene; and protogene begat eozoon, and eozoon begat monad, and monad begat animalculæ.

7. And animalculæ begat ephemra: then began creeping things to multiply on the face of the earth.

8. And earthly atom in protoplasm begat molecule, and thence came grass and every herb of the earth.

9. And animalculæ in the water evolved fins, tails, claws and scales; and in the air wings and beaks: and on the land they sprouted such organs as were necessary as played upon by the environment.

10. And by accretion and absorption, came the radiata and mollusca, and mollusca begat articulata, and articulata begat vertebrate.

11. Now these are the generations of the higher vertebrata in the cosmic period that the Unknowable evoluted the biped mammalia:

12. And every man of the earth, while he was yet a monkey, and the horse, while he was yet the hipparion, and the hipparion before he was an oredon. Out of the ascidian came the amphibian and begat the pentadactyle, and by inheritance and selection, produced the hylobate, from which are the simiade in all their tribes.

13. And out of the simiade the lemur prevailed above his fellow and produced the platyrhine monkey.

14. And the plytyrhine begat the catarrhine, and the catarrhine begat the anthropoid ape and the ape begat the longimanous orang, and the orang begat the chimpanzee, and the chimpanzee evolved the what-is-it?

15. And the what-is-it? went into the land of Nod, and took him a wife of the longimanous gibbons.

16. And in the process of the cosmic period were born unto them their children the anthromorphic premordial types.

17. The homunculus the prognathus; the troglodyte, and the autochthon, the terragon,—these are the generations of primeval man.

18. And primeval man was naked and not ashamed, but lived in quadrumanous innocence, and struggled mightily to harmonize with the environment.

19. And by inheritance and natural selection did he progress from the stable and homogeneous to the complex and the heterogeneous; for the weakest died, and the strongest grew and multiplied.

20. And man grew a thumb for that he had need of, and developed capacities for prey.

21. For behold, the swiftest animals got away from the slow men, wherefore the slow animals were eaten and the slow men starved to death.

22. And as the types differentiated the weaker types continually disappeared.

23. And the earth was filled with violence; for man strove with man, and tribe with tribe, whereby they killed off the weak and foolish and secured "the survival of the fittest."

Moses again appeals to the public, "Choose you this day which you will have"—what the Spirit saith, or what the self-styled Scientist asserteth!

At many points evolution is anti-scriptural. The majority of evolutionists, certainly the most able ones among them, contend for the eternity of matter. The Scriptures assert the opposite. "By faith we understand that the worlds have been framed by the Word of God, so that which is seen hath not been made out of things which appeared." (Heb. 11:3).

Almost to a man, evolutionists contend that species are the product of natural selection. Ten times in the first chapter of Genesis the law "after its own kind" is declared, and it covers every form of life, from the blade of grass to the god-like occupants of Eden. It is little wonder, therefore, that when such men as Crawford H. Toy, George Burnam Foster, B. Fay Mills, and R. J. Campbell adopt the evolution theory *in toto*, that they immediately begin to treat the Word of God as though it were without authority.

And it is hardly to be wondered at that Prof. Haeckel, the most noted evolutionist, should proceed, in his "Riddles of the Universe" to read God out of it altogether. However, there is one thing to be said in favor of these men. They are intelligent enough to see the inharmony between the Scriptures and this present-day popular theory; and honest enough to say, "We prefer evolution to the Book." It is easier to hold such men in esteem than it is to respect those who go up and down the land telling us that evolution is true, and so is the Bible. Such teachers seem to belong with the boy Dr. John Henry Barrows is reported to have met in India. "A native lad had attended the Christian schools and learned there the shape and situation of the earth, but in his Hindoo home he had been taught the Hindoo cosmogony, namely, that the earth was circled by salt water, and that by a circle of earth, and these by successive circles of sweet cane juice and other soft drinks, with intervening circles of land. Dr. Barrows asked the boy which belief he would hereafter hold? He replied that he "would believe both."

THE THEORY AND FALSE THEOLOGY.

The intimate relation between this theory and theology is becoming more and more apparent. It is doubtful if there is a single skeptical professor in the Old World or the New, who is not also a fairly full-fledged evolutionist. The theological result is perfectly evident in such books as "The Finality of the Christian Religion" and the "New Theology."

According to evolutionists, *God is a force,* and those ministers who have accepted the evolutionary theory of the natural universe, have lost their personal heavenly Father in consequence. The shibboleth of such professed Christian preachers is one with that of the atheistic philosophers when they have found a common view-point in evolution. It is a remarkable fact to find Daniel, when he comes to describe the coming Prince who shall oppose God, and magnify himself beyond all, literally saying, "But in his estate he shall honor the god of force." (Dan. 11:38). Are our Critics the forerunners of the antiChrist?

Evolution makes *Christ only a remarkable man.* One calls Him "the only man;" another believes that he was the "mental product of excessive admiration." "The Flower of the Race" is so beautiful an expression, that quite a few of them agree in its adoption. But, whatever the expression, essential deity is never intended, and to admit that He was begotten by the Holy Ghost would introduce supernaturalism, which they repudiate. Foster's astonishment that "Belief in the virgin birth of Jesus should ever have been held as a cardinal article of the Christian faith" is shared by a majority of the Huxleyites.

His resurrection from the dead is either denied outright or else explained away by affirming that it was not physical. His promise to come again at the end of the Age and introduce a millenium wherein He himself shall "reign from sea to sea and from the rivers to the ends of the earth" they repudiate to a man, and so fulfill the prediction of Peter, "In the last days mockers shall come with mockery, walking after their own lusts, and saying, Where is the promise of his coming; for from the day that the fathers fell asleep all things continue as they were from the beginning of creation."

This theory makes sin essentially a virtue. Man is not a fallen creature. One of their best exponents, a good representative of a great university, recently affirmed in my presence that "to tell children they were not by nature children of God, was irrational; to instruct them that the essential thing was the evolution of the life within them, was sanity." To such teachers "sin" is not "a transgression of the law of God," but simply false strokes in the struggle to be free from self-limitations and opposing environments.

While compelled to admit that a crab-apple will never produce pippins unless the latter be grafted in, they yet insist that the child which the Scriptures declares is "conceived in sin and shapen in iniquity" can become a saint without "the grafting in" of the new nature, or the regenerating work of the Holy Ghost. To them, Paul's description of sin as "exceedingly sinful," is without justification, and the prophet's statement "The soul that sinneth it shall die" should be changed to "The soul that sinneth is searching after life."

To be sure some of the greater minds among them do not go to these lengths. Henry Drummond held to the necessity of the new birth, but for that matter, Drummond's "Natural Law in the Spiritual World" is the very antithesis of the full-fledged evolution theory.

The resurrection is even more offensive to evolutionists, than is regeneration. It just as certainly introduces the supernatural, and it brings the work of the Spirit before the natural vision where men can see and judge for themselves. His appearance to "above five hundred brethren at once" (1. Cor. 15:6) is boldly disputed, and the explanation of their testimony is found in the fervor with which these deluded disciples loved their leader.

It makes the cross only a criminal mistake. From their view-point it was not according to prophecy, nor did it in any wise profit the race. It was only a notable one among the many instances where men, actuated by human hatred and selfishness, have ignorantly slain their friend. As a rule, they scoff the notion that "He bore our sins on the tree," and will have none of the teaching that "by the shedding of His blood" we have secured our "remission." Christ crucified, is unto these, as to the Jews of old, "a stumbling block;" and as unto the Gentiles of former times, "foolishness."

To them redemption is a misleading term. The thought of God buying back, with His precious blood, that which man had forfeited to the Adversary is little better than a jest. "Salvation must be by self-development!" they insist. Paul, when he dares to say, "By grace are ye saved, through faith, and that not of yourselves," is simply mistaken.

What then, is the conclusion of the whole matter? Some writer has summed it up after this manner: "A pantheistic god, instead of a personal God. A human savior instead of a divine Savior. Infallible scholarship instead of an infallible Bible. Reformation instead of regeneration. Culture instead of conversion. The natural in all things, the supernatural in nothing." These are the result of modern scholarship! Certainly, as Dr. A. H. Strong, of Rochester Seminary, says: "We need a new vision of the Savior to convince us that Jesus is lifted above space and time, that His existence antedated creation, that He conducted the march of Hebrew history, that He was born of a virgin, suffered on the cross, rose from the dead, and now lives forever more, the Lord of the universe, the only God with whom we have to do, our Savior here and our Judge hereafter. Without a revival of this faith our churches become secularized, mission enterprise will die out and the candlestick will be removed out of its place, as it was in the seven churches of Asia, and as it has been with the apostate churches of New England."

Chapter V.

ARE THE SACRED SCRIPTURES UNSCIENTIFIC?

"Thy word is true from the beginning." (Ps. 119:160.) This is an expression of the Psalmist that must be explained away before one can pit Science and the Sacred Scriptures against each other. Since the purpose of preaching is interpretation of the Word, rather than its annihilation, we shall not attempt either to dispute the veracity of this statement or to spiritualize it into some strange and unnatural explanation. Arthur Pierson thinks the Psalmist meant to say that from the first word the Sacred Scriptures are true.

But the modern method of study objects to any assumption. It insists that every theme and thing shall be subjected to whatever tests are essential in the establishment of its claims. To this, intelligent believers take no exception. If the Bible will not bear investigation; if scrutiny discloses shortcomings; if research disproves its assertions; if true Science discredits its clear claims, let it fall. We could forfeit it without a tear; join in digging its grave without regret, and return to the duties of life smitten by no serious bereavement.

True, it is serious business to discredit a book which has accomplished for the world what the Bible has wrought; but it would be more serious to believe a lie, or even to accept an irresponsible chart in making one's way over the sea of life. True, the Bible "was not written to show how the heavens go;" but rather "how to go to heaven;" it is not a text book on science, but a guide-book for godly living. And yet, when it addresses itself at all to a subject of scientific concern, it should speak the truth, if it makes the claim of inspiration! When we study the words of men, however wise they may be, we expect to come upon mistake. When we read, and properly understand, what "God hath spoken" we anticipate no such results. "Let God be found true; but every man a liar." "He that believeth not God hath made him a liar."

"But," we are told, "God has two books. One we call 'Nature,' the other 'Revelation;' that He is just as certainly the author of the former as of the latter; that one is the work of His hands and the other the fruit of His lips." What Jesus, when once he stooped down and wrote in the sand, expressed, we do not know. But can any man imagine that His writings in the sand were out of harmony with His spoken addresses, and is it possible that an all-wise God has produced in Nature and in Revelation contradictory volumes?

We have no fear whatever that the Scriptures must be maintained at the expense of Science; and we are equally persuaded that true Science will never be established at the cost of Scripture. The thing to be feared is, that the dust of false reasoning (of which the air is full today) will get into the eyes of men, and make it impossible for one to read from the Sacred Page, and for another to see the meaning of the open book of Nature; and so for either, to discern the perfect agreement between God's Word and God's Work.

First or all, then, let us give

THE DEFINITION OF THE TERMS INVOLVED.

What is Science? Can we improve upon the Standard Dictionary's statement—"Knowledge gained and verified by exact observation and correct thinking; especially as methodically formulated and arranged in a rational system?" That definition takes you at once out of the realm of speculation. It disposes of such terms as "theory" and "hypothesis," making them possible servants of Science, but never its synonym. It is everywhere admitted that almost every assertion made in the name of Science a hundred years since, is now out of date; and while this clearly demonstrates our progress, it also suggests that we are still in the hypothetical and theoretical stage. No one would dispute that Sir Isaac Newton was somewhat of a scientist, nor yet that Tyndall was equally worthy the name, and yet when they take exactly opposite positions concerning the refraction of light, both may be wrong, but both cannot be right. Huxley and Darwin are names that somehow sit easily together in the same sentence, and yet these men, working in almost the same realm, are not always in agreement. The explanation is easy—"the verification of knowledge by exact observation and correct thinking" is the highest accomplishment of which the human mind is capable, and not every man who cries "Eureka" has found it. This is not to inveigh against the sincerity of investigators, nor even to deride their conclusions, but only to call attention to the most patent fact of their experience! "Knowledge gained and verified by exact observation and correct thinking" will never be overthrown by mortal men, nor yet by God. God would dethrone Himself by such an endeavor!

What is Scripture? Paul defines "all Scripture" as that which is "God-breathed," and the process of it is "that holy men of old spake as they were moved (or borne along) by the Holy Ghost!" Knowing himself to be of that company, Paul affirms, "We speak not in words which man's wisdom teacheth, but which the Spirit teacheth; combining spiritual things with spiritual words." If one runs through the Old Testament he will find God everywhere assuming the Authorship of the Sacred Scriptures. The phrases are like these: "The Lord spake unto Moses saying, etc." "These are the words of the covenant which the Lord commanded Moses to make with the children of Israel." "The Lord spake unto Joshua." "The words of the commandment of the Lord." Not scores, but hundreds of times, does God claim to be the Author both of thought and language in the Holy Book. David declares, "The Spirit of the Lord spake by me, and his word was in my tongue." (2 Samuel 23:2.) To me it is the most remarkable evidence of the skepticism of the age that because there are some difficulties in the theory of Verbal Inspiration men are willing to throw it away, and adopt such notions as are now current, to the effect that God simply stimulated the thought, but did not determine the speech; that some parts of the Bible are literally true, and others are only allegory; that some are fact, others only fiction; that some are to be treated with credence and others with criticism; that all must come to the test of one's "inner consciousness," and at that court be either accepted or rejected.

The same men who so define "Inspiration" or "Illumination" or whatever it is, would go into court tomorrow to insist upon the settlement of an estate, in which they were named as heirs, on a *verbal basis*. They would call the attention of attorneys and judge to what was "written," and unless they had some unrighteous end to be conserved, they would permit no departure from *the very words* in which the testator had expressed himself. It is little wonder, therefore, that the New Testament writers, who may be conceded to have known what the Scriptures were, refer to the Old Testament more than eighty times, as that "which is written." Never once did they abandon the literal interpretation of the same.

If the words of the Old Testament were "the words of God," perhaps no believer, at least, will dispute that the New Testament stands upon the same level. And so the Bible does not "contain the Scriptures;" the Bible is the Scriptures,—God's revealed Word, which can hardly have been given to men with less care than any intelligent, faithful father would show in framing the article that bequeathed his possessions to his children. If, in civil courts, the lightest word of the testator is the weightiest law, who will dare to treat with contempt, thought or phrase found in the Divine Will?

Mark you, there is a decided difference between the plain statement of the Sacred Scriptures and some absurd opinion. It may be, that in the centuries of the past an uninstructed Christian conceived the world as having a flat surface, the sky as a roof and the stars as holes through the same. Kepler, who was something of a scientist, once expressed the conviction that the world was a living animal. Is that assertion to be confounded with Science? Fanciful interpretations in the one realm are just as common as in the other; and they neither prove nor disprove anything. I do not have to harmonize the Scriptures with the absurd statements of every man who may speak in the name of Science; and I do not have to harmonize Science with the assertions of every man who may mistakenly appeal to Moses, or even to Christ. Science is God's voice in Nature; the Scriptures are God's voice in grace, and it does not fall to the lot of any mortal man to harmonize them; the harmony is in Him. He cannot contradict Himself!

To say the least, it is a strange procedure when a man proclaims as his theme "The Harmony between Science and Scripture" and then shows how that comes to pass by just quietly disposing of the latter; by saying, for instance, that the first chapter of Genesis is "the best that Moses knew,—the impression of that early age, but a mistake none the less." Is that harmony? Is it not rather, annihilation? It may let you out of your difficulty, but you escape at the expense of inspiration; and to the unspeakable loss of the people. There used to be an eccentric preacher in Kentucky well-known to the author. He did no great amount of study, and yet he commonly preached with unction. One day he found himself before an audience with no unction on hand; even thoughts refused to come. He floundered through a few ill-formed sentences, and then, squarely facing his audience, he said, "Brethren and sisters, you think I have gotten into the brush, and can't get out, don't you? Well, I'll show you; we'll just look to the Lord and be dismissed." But let it be understood that when you dismiss the claims of the Sacred Book, and walk out of your difficulties, you have lost the divine message and left the hungry multitudes unsatisfied.

GENESIS IN SCIENCE AND SCRIPTURE.

It will scarcely be disputed that so far as men have seen any inharmony between the Sacred Scriptures and Science, the first chapter of Genesis has been made the storm center. On that account I invite your athtention to this part of the Word, and dare the assertion that its careful study, instead of demonstrating the inharmony between Science and Scripture, will reveal the most undreamed of agreement in these great books of God.

First of all, *think of the argument from fifteen facts in order.*

First fact, in order,—God created the heavens.

Second fact, in order—"and the earth;" third—water; fourth—light; fifth—firmament; sixth—grass; seventh—herb; eighth—tree; ninth—appearance of heavenly bodies; tenth—fish; eleventh—moving things; twelfth—fowls; thirteenth—creeping things; fourteenth—cattle; fifteenth—man.

Now, the latest science will consent to this order of creation. The heavens were certainly made first; the earth certainly came second; water certainly appeared third, light—fourth; firmament—next; grass thereafter; the manifestation of sun and moon—ninth; the appearance of fish—tenth; moving things—eleventh; fowls—twelfth; creeping things—thirteenth; cattle, etc., fourteenth, and last, man.

Other writers have called attention to the unspeakable significance of this order when considered before the law of permutation. The Standard Dictionary says, "The number of permutations of any given number of things, taken all at a time, is equal to the product of the natural numbers from one up to the number given, inclusive."

Now if Moses only spake the science of his times, he knew practically nothing of the order of creation. Consequently he must guess at it. He must guess whether the heavens or the earth were first formed. In his day no man imagined that the heavenly bodies were bigger than the earth, and all men supposed that they moved about it. How then does it happen that Moses, when he came to guess which was first formed, the heavens or the earth, mentioned the heavens in the primary place? You say, "Well it was an easy accident, since there was only one other alternative." Did you ever hear the story of the Irishman who, meeting a neighbor said, "We have a fine baby at our house this marning; guiss whither it is a boy or a gurl?" "A girl," said the neighbor." "No, Sir, guiss agin." "Well, I say a boy!" "Well, neow, who tole you?" To be

THE HIGHER CRITICISM. 103

sure Moses had one chance out of two on this arrangement. But he got it right!

Third fact—the appearance of water. Here Moses' task was not so easy, for it was not one in three, but one in six, according to the law of permutation. It could have been, the heavens first, water second, earth third, but that was not true; it could have been, the earth first, water second, and the heavens third, but that was not true. It could have been water first, the earth second, and the heavens last, but that was not true. It could have been the earth first, the heavens second and water last, but that was not true. In other words there are six different arrangements of these relations, 1-2-3, 1-3-2; 2-1-3, 2-3-1; 3-2-1; 3-1-2. But Moses somehow struck the right one. A good guesser! Introduce light and you make twenty-four such relations. But Moses hit it again. One chance in twenty-four, but he was the lucky man.

When you get the fifth you have 120 possible orders. Strange to say Moses does not miss it!

When you get to the sixth, you have 720. In other words there are 719 chances against you. But Moses got it right!

When you get to the seventh, you have 5,040. In other words 5,039 chances against you. But Moses hit it!

When you get to the eighth you have 40,320. Not a glorious prospect of striking it straight, but still Moses accomplishes it!

When you get to the ninth you only have one chance in 362,880.

When you get to the tenth, you have only one chance in 3,628,800!

When you get to the eleventh, 39,916,800.

When you get to the fifteenth, one chance in 1,307,674,367,900. And yet, strange to say, in the whole arrangement, he never misses!

Go dig up Bob Ingersoll, and give the poor fellow a chance to apologize for ever having spoken of the "mistakes of Moses." Bob should not come alone!

But this is not the end. We make bold to assert that from the beginning to the end of Genesis, 1st Chapter, there is not a scientific *mistake*. It is scientific that the heavens were created first, and the earth second. The very latest Science would tell you that the earth was "waste and void," and the "darkness," resulting from the nebulous state, "was upon the face of the deep." For a long time Science spoke of the third verse as certainly involving a mistake, "And God said, Let there be light and there was light." This, in advance of the appearance of the sun or moon. They supposed that the sun was the only source of light, but finally Laplace declared it to be a scientific certainty, that in the condensation of the originally formless chaos, there was such molecular and chemical action as must have emitted light. No wonder Boardman, in his "Creative Week," says, "Why will the Academy vote Moses a blunderer for declaring that light existed before the sun appeared, and yet vote Laplace a scientist for affirming precisely the same thing?"

The next point of scientific attack was upon the fifth verse, "And there was evening, and there was morning, one day." It was boldly asserted that Moses supposed all this change from chaos to cosmos took place in twenty-four hours. But mark you, Moses does not refer to twenty-four hours at all! "From evening to morning" is only twelve hours. You will not have finished this chapter until it is made perfectly clear that Moses is not speaking of twenty-four hour days. He knew the law of herbs, yielding seed after their kind, and trees bearing fruit after their kind," that these things were not accomplished in a day; that it took seasons to produce fruit, and even many years, to mature trees and make them reproductive. And yet that whole process he mentions as in the third day. What is God's Day, according to the Bible? In the second chapter the entire creation, from start to finish, is mentioned as having occurred in a day. It could not, therefore, according to Moses, mean twenty-four hours. *What is a "yom" with God?* Peter tells us "One day is with the Lord as a thousand years." (2 Pet. 3:8). Moses, himself, in the ninetieth Psalm, declares that "a thousand years in God's sight were but as yesterday when it is passed, and as a watch in the night," and that he is speaking of this very period is evident in the context, where he says, "Before the mountains were brought forth and thou gavest birth to the earth and the world, even from everlasting to everlasting (from Olan to Olam: or, era to era), thou art God."

But surely Moses was mistaken in the eighth verse, "And God called the firmament heaven?" Even Mr. Huxley slipped here, by charging Moses with believing that heaven was a solid substance, resting like a canopy over the earth. But Mr. Huxley was not a Hebrew scholar; hence his mistake. The Hebrew word translated "firmament" means "expanse." Can you beat it by your latest scientific expression?

The ninth verse also reveals the remarkable wisdom vouchsafed to this man, "Let the waters under the heaven be gathered together in one place, and let the dry land appear." There was not a man in the earth at that time that knew, or could have known, that all the seas were linked together, whereas the continents are divided. But exploration has proven it. Dana, in his Manual of Geology, says that while the continents are separated, the seas occupy one bed. As to the order of the appearance of life, Genesis and geology are exactly together, beginning with grass, and ending with man. There is not a geological mistake in Genesis.

Equally remarkable is the fact that instead of speaking of the sun and moon as giving their light from the first, Moses holds back their rays until the fourth day; at which time he does not declare they were created, for that belonged in the opening sentence, "In the beginning God created the heavens"—but they were made to "divide the day from the night, "and to be for signs and for seasons and for days and for years." Many scientists believe that the earth took on its present angle of axis at this very period in its development, when it cooled to the point where the vapors condensed and fell upon it as water. And we know that without that axis-angle, determining its relation to the sun and moon, our seasons would fail, and we would return to an ice-age!

Now as to whether the law of generation, as set forth in Genesis, "every seed after its kind" is true, or whether the origin of species is by "natural selection," the whole weight of discovery is with Genesis and against Darwin. The truth of Genesis we know, from the lowest form of grass to soulful man; everything is bringing forth "after its kind." We have seen that law executed ten thousands times and in millions of forms. The creation of a new species, by natural selection, no man has ever yet seen. Why, therefore, should we imagine that there is any conflict between Scripture and Science? At every point where it is possible to institute a comparison that is reliable, an utter agreement appears! The rocks, from the lowest strata to the last laid down, confirm the facts of God's creative week.

> "A Glory guilds the Sacred page
>   Majestic like the sun,
> It gives a light to every age,
>   It gives but borrows none.
>
> The hand that gave it still supplies
>   The gracious light and heat:
> His truths upon the nations rise;
>   They rise, but never set."

Permit me to mention some other *inexplicable instances of Science in Scripture*. Harvey, in modern times, discovered the circulation of the blood, and declared its relation to life. Moses affirmed it three thousand years ago—"The life is in the blood." You have heard Galileo glorified for having discovered that this part of the universe was heliocentric and not geocentric, as the ancients supposed; and Newton honorably mentioned for his great discovery of the law of gravitation. The Scriptures declared both a few thousand years before these brethren were born. Job declared of the day-spring, that it "takes hold of the ends of the earth; it is turned as clay to the seal" (38-13), and as for gravitation, while scientists and churchmen alike were adopting theories of the earth's support, akin to that which the Hindus now hold, namely, that it was a flat plane, with possible stories above and below, held up by the heads of elephants, with their tails turned out, and their feet resting on the shell of an immense tortoise, and the tortoise in turn on the coil of a snake, Job was remonstrating in these words, "He hangeth the earth upon nothing," (26:7)—the very deliverance of your latest Science!

It is only in very modern times that any man imagined the atmosphere to have any weight, and we still employ the phrase, "light as air" and yet we know that it has a weight of fifteen pounds to every square inch; and modern science could almost tell you exactly what was the awful pressure upon the face of the globe twenty-five thousand miles in circumference. This, however, was not information to the Old Testament writers! Job, one of the most ancient of them all, says of God, that "he makes a weight for the wind; yea, he meeteth out the waters by measure." Galileo discovered that air has gravity; but thirty centuries before him Job affirmed the same. It would seem, therefore, that inspiration is as accurate as experimentation.

It is only within a few years that weather bureaus have had any occasion; that men imagined storms of cloud and wind, and waves of heat and cold obeyed unchangeable laws, and might, therefore, be tabulated and reported even in advance of their arrival. But Solomon understood it and wrote long since, in Ecclesiastes 1:6, "The wind goeth toward the south and turneth about unto the north. It turneth about continually in its course, and the wind returneth again to its circuits." It is only by modern discoveries that men imagined that there were other sounds than those which our ears catch; but now we know that when we pass thirty-eight thousand vibrations per second, the ear cannot follow, and every heavenly body, in its motions, is making music, so that Job was not mistaken when he declared "the morning stars sang together," nor David when he declared of Jehovah, "Thou makest the morning and the evening to rejoice."

Arthur Pierson, after-having called attention

to some of these remarkable instances of agreement, says Shakespeare was right when he wrote:

"There's not the smallest orb which thou beholdest,
But in his motion, like an angel sings,
Still choiring to the young-eyed cherubim.
Such harmony is in immortal souls;
But whilst this muddy vesture of decay
Doth grossly close it in, we cannot hear it."

We candidly believe that if the men who are spending much time in seeing what can be said against the Scriptures, should assume a friendly attitude and search with a kindred diligence for its remarkable defenses, they could find them with utter ease, and would be shortly confirmed in the "faith once delivered" and able to boast with the poet:

"I paused one day beside the blacksmith's door
And listened to the anvil ring the evening's chime.
And looking in I saw upon the floor,
Old hammers, worn with beating years of time."

'How many anvils have you had,' said I,
'To wear and batter out these hammers so?'
'Just one,' he answered, with a twinkling eye,
'The anvil wears the hammers out, you know.'"

"And so, I thought, the Anvil of God's Word
For ages skeptic blows have beat upon;
Yet, though the noise of infidel was heard
The anvil is unworn, the hammers gone!"

SOME POINTS WHERE COMPARISON IS IMPOSSIBLE.

Not to all subjects to which Science speaks do the Scriptures address themselves. It is equally true that the Scriptures discuss many subjects with which Science has naught to do. There are points in human experience where the microscope, the scalpel, the telescope tell us nothing. They transcend all scientific investigation! Tyndall admitted that the problem of the universe would probably never be solved! And yet that problem is not more difficult than are the problems of sin, substitution and salvation.

A man may easily say that Moses was mistaken when he declared how sin came into the world. But who will attempt to demonstrate it and how? We know that sin is here. The Bible affirms that it came through an evil spirit; that man accepted his suggestion and continues to accept it, and so suffers the penalty of violated law. Who has presented a saner explanation of sin?

It is the height of folly to speak of "the Scriptures as teaching that the innocent must suffer for the sins of the guilty," "that children are condemned because of their parents' blunder." It never hints such a thing, and it never did. The second commandment does not say that God is visiting the iniquities of the fathers upon their innocent children, but it does affirm that "judgment falls upon the third and fourth generation of them that hate him," and why shouldn't it, unto generations of generations? Shall men hate God and escape judgment? The law, when first declared was, "The soul that sinneth it shall die." Is not that law righteous? The Scriptures are very careful to follow that statement with another from the pen of Ezekiel, "The son shall not bear the iniquity of the father; neither shall the father bear the iniquity of the son. The righteousness of the righteous shall be upon him; and the wickedness of the wicked shall be upon him."

It may be easy enough to set up untenable theories of sin, and assign them either to the Sacred Scriptures, or to the conservative defenders of the same, when neither have ever spoken aught to warrant such caricature. I have been in the ministry for twenty-six years. My daily associations, of an intrinsic character, have been with the conservative wing of the church, and in that entire time I have never heard Jehovah described as a God who visited the sins of guilty parents upon the heads of innocent children, by any one of them. On the contrary, they have depicted Jehovah as a God of infinite love, punishing no innocent men or women; even pitying the sinner and proffering him grace in Jesus Christ. Will the man who sets himself up as a student of Science, and a preacher of the Sacred Scriptures, object; and, if so, has he a better view of God to present?.

Again, if the God who breathed upon the waste of a darkened world, and converted its chaos into cosmos, and quickened its death into life, is willing to do the same for a man "dead in trespasses and sins," will men object, or the scientist dispute His right? Cannot He of whom Milton sang, saying,

"Thou from the first
Wast present, and with mighty wings outstretch-
    ed,
Dove-like, sat'st brooding on the vast abyss,
And madest it pregnant,"

quicken our dead souls that they shall live again? If we cannot bind the influences of the Pleiades, shall we attempt to set limits to the work of God's own Spirit, or demand that He bring His endeavors within the limits of natural explanation?

Is it not written, "Except one be born of water and the Spirit, he cannot enter into the Kingdom of God. And that which is born of the flesh is flesh; and that which is born of the Spirit is spirit," and are we not enjoined to "marvel not" about it, since "the wind bloweth where it will, and thou hearest the voice thereof, but knowest not whence it cometh and whither it goeth," and told, "so is every one that is born of the Spirit?" Just how it happens that the drunken man who staggers into a sanctuary and listens to the Gospel of the Son of God, and goes out, never to drink again, supported, in his new sobriety, by the sense of Divine love, Science may never be able to explain; but that does not disprove what you and I have seen.

Just how it happens that the woman who has walked in the ways of wickedness, is suddenly roused to repentance by the rehearsal of the divine goodness, scientists may not even see, but the Son of Man rejoices and the angels are made happy by the sight of His face. You can deny the direct creation of man in the divine image if you like, but you will never be able to disprove it. You may deny the unity of the race, but even there the evidences are against you; you may deny the description of the fall, but sin remains unexplained. You may deny that there is any supernaturalism and yet, as against that, we say that he who starts along the path clearly marked in Sacred Scripture will go from sin to salvation; from salvation to sanctification, and from sanctification to the eternal fellowship of the Father.

Years ago we went through the Hoosac Tunnel for the first time. Did you ever hear how it was constructed? There started two companies of men to work on opposite sides of the mountain, but the survey had been so accurately made that when the men met midway, the walls of the excavations were not an inch off the line. But the man who wants to turn home to God and heaven has more than an accurate line marked by survey; he has a well-beaten road lying full before him. Others have gone over it by the thousands; yea, by the millions, and as the prodigal who trudged his way back to the farm house, from which he had been so long separated, by a well-traveled road, found his Father coming forth to meet him, so shall the lost man find God if he but turn his feet to the path upon which there falls the light of this Word!

Chapter VI.

THE FINALITY OF THE HIGHER CRITCISM.

"I charge thee in the sight of God, and of Christ Jesus, who shall judge the living and the dead, and by his appearing and his kingdom: preach the word: be urgent in season, out of season; reprove, rebuke, exhort, with all long suffering and teaching. For the time will come when they will not endure sound doctrine; but, having itching ears, will heap to themselves teachers after their own lusts; and will turn away their ears from the truth, and turn aside unto fables." (2 Tim. 4:1-4).

When one reads the epistles of John he is profoundly impressed with the thought that the Spirit of God anticipated some of the most hurtful heresies of these latter times and answered them entirely, two thousand years before they were born; such, for instance, as the unscriptural doctrine of "Perfectionism" preached in some parts, and that masterpiece of Satan, "Christian Science," and its allied movements, "Spiritualism," "Theosophy," "New Thought," etc. Paul, as a contributor to the New Testament exceeds even John, and while there is scarcely any error of doctrine or practice which he passes over without reproof, he was peculiarly employed by the Spirit of God to anticipate and reprove attacks to be made upon "the Word of God." Our text is only one of many which the great Apostle addresses to this evident end.

Any natural interpretation of this text makes it applicable to the subject in hand, namely, "The Finality of the Higher Criticism."

In glancing the text through we call your attention to four of its suggestions—The Higher Criticism and the Word; The Higher Criticism and the War; Higher Criticism and Apostasy and Higher Criticism as a Propaganda.

HIGHER CRITICISM AND THE WORD.

"Preach the Word." The great questions of the present controversy, in the theological world, are these, "What is the Word?" and "What of the Word?" "Is the Bible a divinely inspired message?" "Are its historical statements reliable?" "Is its moral code binding?"

To all of these questions Higher Criticism addresses itself. We propose to bring you its answers from a man who is regarded in many quarters as a radical; and yet from a book which comes more nearly revealing not alone the concept and custom of this critical method, but its final and logical conclusions, than any other put forth up to the present. We refer to George Burman Foster's volume, "The Finality of the Christian Religion."

According to it, these three assertions will not be disputed: (1) Higher Criticism denies the inspiriation of the Word. (2) Higher Criticism disputes the reliability of the Word. (3) Higher Criticism rejects the authority of the Word.

Higher Criticism denies the inspiration of the Word. On page 63 Dr. Foster says, "The doctrine of the inspiration of the Scriptures .... is of pagan origin." And on page 87 the author asserts that the doctrine of Verbal Inspiration was first given up, then inspiration as a divine guidance in the writing down of what was supernaturally revealed was surrendered; that the next step was to think of it as "a mere negative protection from error;" but it was impossible to stop there, and so they concluded that this protection referred only to the "religious content." But since the "religious content" was often but the work of mortal men, it was decided that "only Jesus was inerrant;" and then that His inerrancy applied only to the "region of religious truth." But, as if even this was too great a concession for the Critics to make, Dr. Foster remarks, "The inspiration of the Book is untrue historically and impossible psychologically."

Higher Criticism disputes the reliability of the Word. This is the inevitable result of logic. Without a divine inspiration it is impossible that the Scriptures should be reliable. Dr. Foster accepts that consequence and carries the result to its inevitable end, affirming that even Jesus took on the form attributed to Him in the New Testament through "emotional reconstruction." (p. 396.) His infatuated followers "dehumanized and spiritualized Him." Their affectionate feelings for Jesus went so far that "no man can tell where facts end and embellishment of facts begins," (p. 396). Adding to this argument, losses sustained by translation from one language to another, Dr. Foster concludes, "We do not surely know that we have any strictly authentic words of Jesus." (p. 400).

If the New Testament writers, who were confessedly eye-witnesses of the historical facts of Christ's life, are incapacitated to write the truth by reason of their ardent admiration of the Man of Nazareth, and what they have written may not be known to us because of the difficulties of translation, how much more unreliable is the entire Old Testament, which deals in many instances with ages to which the writers did not belong, and has reached us by a process of translation fraught with far greater dangers?

There is another, and natural step to be taken, and notwithstanding the gravity of its consequences, it is accepted by the Critics.

Higher Criticism rejects the authority of the Word. Dr. Foster goes so far as to affirm that "there is no evidence up to 150 A. D. that any New Testament writers were supposed to be even sacred." (p. 106). He asserts, "There does not seem to be any passage of literature in the sub-apostolic generation that warrants the conclusion that an apostolic letter was appealed to as a sacred writing." To be sure, the Doctor is a metaphysician rather than a student of Sacred Writ, and he may be excused for his ignorance of what Peter wrote in his second epistle, 3:15-16, quoting from Paul, and referring to " the *wisdom* given him." "Wherefore, beloved, seeing that ye look for these things, give diligence that ye may be found in peace, without spot and blameless in his sight. And account that the long suffering of our Lord is salvation; even as our beloved brother Paul also, according to the wisdom given him, wrote unto you; as also in all his epistles, speaking in them of these things, wherein are some things hard to be understood, which the ignorant and unsteadfast wrest, as they do also the other scriptures, unto their own destruction."

And yet, the men who deny the inspiration of the Word, dispute its reliability and reject its authority are not altogether willing to give it up, retiring it to some shelf of neglect, and treating it as obsolete. Somehow or other, often having slain it, they are loath to lay it away. We wonder whether, after all, if they are not a little alarmed lest, if they did this, the world might lose its moral light, and the much boasted Reason, in which they have trusted, return to its groveling as it has done in those parts of Italy and Spain where priests and Pope have taken the Bible from the people, and in Mexico and Cuba and South America, where Reason has been untrammeled by any special knowledge of the Word, and even, as in fair France, where the goddess of Reason was enthroned one hundred years ago, to witness the immediate Reign of Terror. Henry Rogers, in his "Eclipse of Faith," hints what would happen were the Critics successful and the Bible once for all flung away by men. He records a dream entitled, "The Blank Bible," in which the world had awakened one morning to discover that every copy of the Sacred Scriptures in all the earth had been suddenly withdrawn from among men, and blank books left in their stead. And then he depicts the disappointment of the unsaved that even the way of salvation no longer existed for them; the deprivation of old age that it no longer had the promises upon which to pillow its head; the universal anxiety concerning coming morals, and so on. Dr. Arthur Pierson, speaking to this reputed dream says, 'What if every Bible should turn to blank paper, and all that other books have borrowed from it vanish likewise! What if all that it has wrought in man and for man could be obliterated from human character and history!—all ideas and ideals of chastity and charity, equity and ethics, mercy and magnanimity; all the motives for morality and piety, heroism and martyrdom, which it has supplied!" Who can conceive the wreck and ruin that would reach into every heart and home, church and community? And yet such is the logical process of Higher Criticism. If its conclusions were accepted today, the scene in the streets of Ephesus would necessarily be re-enacted, and the works of those who practiced the magical art of imposing "myths" and "mistakes" upon men in the name of inspiration, would be burned to white-ash in the sight of all. Are the Critics ready to take the responsibility of such a procedure? Yet wherein is the difference between heaping your Bibles in one colossal pile and firing them, and accepting the conclusions of a George Burman Foster? To some of us, at least, the process of firing were far preferable to the retention of a book whose claims of heavenly birth are false, whose commands are only the invention of men, whose supposed historical records are simply myths, or at the most a combination of fact and fancy; and whose plan of salvation, culminating in a Christ—the sinner's substitute—is purely a delusion.

But we are not fully convinced that such is our dilemma, for our text speaks to another subject, namely,

HIGHER CRITICISM AND THE WAR.

"Preach the word; be urgent in season, out of season; reprove, rebuke, exhort, with all long-suffering and teaching." It is just possible that this procedure is not out of date; it is just possible that Paul is a better instructor than Foster; it is just possible that we have a right to pit this ancient scholar, who was converted from infidelity to "the faith that is in Christ" against "the modern man" who has turned from Christ to the infidelity of Rationalism; and that "reproof," "rebuke" and "instruction" are not out of place for even a Higher Critic.

To be sure, Higher Criticism seriously objects to this procedure.

It excites controversy but expects exemption from reproof. There was a time when our Critics were not much given to controversy. All that they claimed for their effusions was "a series of tentative suggestions." Even now they are careful to employ suave speech, and condone the offense of denying inspiration by enconiums on the "moral majesty" of Jesus; and the "superior literary character" of some of the sixty-six books. Their procedure reminds an English writer of the executioner who bowed down before Charles I, kissed his hand, and begged his pardon for the unpleasant business in which he was engaged, but nevereless beheaded him straightway. Referring to the incident Dr. George Lorimer reminds us that today "Infidelity, wearing a mask and uttering courtly words, is sharpening the axe with which to take off the head of Christianity." If Dr. Foster is to be accepted, the Head of Christianity is off already. And yet when he is reproved he whines; when he is told he has no place in an evangelical pulpit or an evangelical denomination he is offended;

and his defenders stand up in their pulpits on the following Sunday and affirm that "if his opposers dared they would burn him at the stake." It is too bad that a man who occupies a University chair must be reproved by his brethren; and yet if Peter in his impetuosity resented the first arrest and crucifixion of Jesus, perhaps the modern believer may be pardoned for refusing to stand by in silence while the risen Christ is "crucified afresh and put to an open shame."

It raises a rebellion, but objects to any rebuke. "Rebellion" is the word we mean to employ, for these men are no longer aliens; they are in the camp. They insist upon retaining the uniform of Christ's army. They take the banner of Jesus, inscribed with His name, and bear it above their own heads. They, like Absalom, while swearing loyalty to the government of the king, are industriously seeking the disaffected and organizing against the day of the king's overthrow. Why should they object to rebuke? Conservatives have not provoked this controversy. These Goliaths have been bestirring themselves and have been saying, "Come to us and we will give thy carcasses to the birds." While a stone from a sling does not feel good, David is not altogether to blame when he answers the challenge. Is the householder who refuses to have his house spoiled to be regarded ungracious and even contentious? Is the student who takes his stand before the door of his library and objects to having people purloin volumes at their pleasure to be condemned as having incited battle? Is the Christian believer, who rebukes a critic that would tear his Bible into shreds and dump the remainder into the ash heap, to be written down as intolerant and the ash heap, to be written down as intolerant and charged with mental martyrdom? To be sure it is a free country, and yet there may be some limit to license. Dr. Dixon tells the story of a man who was taking his gymnastic exercises on the public street. As he widely flung his arms he struck the nose of a passer-by. Instantly the fellow landed a blow at the base of the ear. When the athlete complained that this was "a free country" and he ought to be permitted to take his gymnastics at his pleasure, it was rejoined, "It is a free country; but where my nose begins your liberty ends." The believer regards the Bible as valuable above any individual life; and a blow against it is a deeper wound than can be inflicted upon his person. The man, therefore, who makes this attack, should understand forever that he must expect rebuke. Timothy cannot easily turn truant to his commission, and he is commanded to "Guard the sacred oracles." In the opinion of Conservatives at least, the epistle of Jude is still inspired and by him they are exhorted to "contend earnestly for the faith which was once for all delivered unto the saints."

It essays to teach, but resents conservative exhortation. "Exhort, with all longsuffering and teaching." Dr. Foster argues (p. 163) that as the fathers were mistaken in their interpretations of the faith, and opposed the progress of science, so are their sons doing. He likens the position of the Conservatives to that of the ecclesiastics who persecuted Galileo; to the opinion of John Calvin that the "heavens, sun and moon move about the earth;" and to the notion of Fromundus that if the earth rotated "buildings would fly off with such rapid motion that men would have to be provided with claws, like cats, to enable them to hold fast to the earth's surface." But the Doctor forgets that one can go back into so-called science and recall even more ludicrous mistakes. When did we learn that the world was not on a turtle's back, or borne by the shoulders of Atlas? If the interpreters of the Scriptures made mistakes, and they did, what about the interpretations of the so-called science of the present? What science of twenty-five years ago is still retained in all of its particulars? If the mistakes of past theologians are to be thrown into the faces of the present-day Biblical scholars, are the mistakes of metaphysicians and so-called scientists of yesterday to be ignored in the question of the present time shibboleth? If the Rationalists who dethrone God and repudiate the Scriptures in France, see a reign of terror in flagrant lusts, disintegration of life and society, can a professor—David Schmidt, of Cornell, stand up today and tell us that "Christianity has failed to adapt itself to the spiritual needs of man;" "that the supernatural in religion is foolishness;" "there is no throne beyond;" "no life," and the world escape the bitter fruits of such folly—formulated in the name of science? It is nothing short of desecration of this good term "science" when men put it to such uses. "The heavens declare the glory of God; and the firmament showeth His handiwork." Neither in the one nor the other is there a solitary conflict with the faith revealed in Sacred Writ.

> "In Regions here they all rejoice
> And utter forth a glorious voice,
> Forever singing as they shine
> The hand that made us is Divine."

THE HIGHER CRITICISM AS AN APOSTASY.

"The time will come when they will not endure sound doctrine, but, having itching ears, will heap to themselves teachers after their own lusts."

It is an apostasy from sound doctrine. At every single point—fundamental to the faith of the believer—Higher Criticism parts company with the Scriptures. The Bible says, "Sin is the transgression of the law." Foster says, "Sin is error; a defect in knowledge." (p. 187). The Bible teaches that our salvation inheres in Christ's substitution, "He bare our sins in his own body on the tree." Foster says, "Salvation consists in rectification of knowledge." The Bible insists that sound doctrine is essential to our sanctification. "Sanctify them through thy truth; thy word is truth." Foster says, "The thing to be set right is not a set of ideas but the bent of the will. The agency to be employed is not now 'sound doctrine' so much as sound personality." The Bible puts into the lips of Jesus these words, "No man cometh unto the father but by me." Foster repudiates it by saying, "God is as good as Jesus. Then we may have the faith which the gospel requires—faith in God the Father, in his fatherly grace in forgiving sins, and in an eternal life." (p. 518).

It is an answer to those "having itching ears." But having "itching ears will heap to themselves teachers after their own lusts." The world is full of people who want to hear some new thing. The fact that Higher Criticism is a novelty is its chief attraction. George Ade is much given to slang, but he often expresses the soundest philosophy in the same. In his fable, "The Preacher who Flew His Kite" he hits off this weakness of human nature. (The capitals are Ade's.) A particular parson was conscious that "he was not making a hit with his congregation;" and he knew that "there must be something wrong with his Talk." He had been trying to talk "in a clear and straightforward Manner, omitting Foreign Quotations" and putting up for illustrations "such Historical Characters as were familiar to his Hearers, putting the stubby Old English words ahead of the Latin, and rather flying low along the Intellectual Plane of the Aggregation that chipped in to pay his salary. But the Pew-Holders were not tickled. They could Understand everything he said, and they began to think he was Common." So he studied the situation and on the Sunday morning following "got up in the Lookout and read a text that didn't mean anything." "Then he sized up his Flock with a Dreamy Eye and said: 'We cannot more

adequately voice the Poetry and Mysticism of our Text than in those familiar Lines of the great Icelandic Poet, Ikon Navrojik:'
"To hold is not to have—
Under the seared Firmament,
Where Chaos sweeps, and Vast Futurity
Sneers at these puny Aspirations—
There is the full Reprisal."

"When the Preacher concluded this Extract from the Well-Known Icelandic Poet, he paused and looked downward, breathing heavily through his Nose, like Camille in the Third Act." The venerable harness dealer was nodding approvingly. "Having wiped his brow, he took a turn at Quarolius, who he claimed had "disputed the Contention of the great Persian Theologian Ramtazuk, that the Soul, in its reaching out after the Unknowable, was guided by the Scriptural Genesis of Motive rather than by mere Impulse of Mentality." Ade says, "The Preacher didn't know what all This meant, and he didn't care." But the pew-holders were "On in a minute." "He talked it off in just the Way that Cyrano talks when he gets Roxane so Dizzy that she nearly falls off the Piazza." Quoting copiously from "the Great Poet Amebius" and reciting "eighteen lines of Greek" and then growing more versatile still, he illustrated from the "Celebrated Poet of Ecuador" and rose to a climax by getting "rid of long Boston Words that hadn't been used before that Season." "He grabbed a rhetorical Roman Candle in each Hand and you couldn't see him for the Sparks." After this he "sank his Voice to a Whisper and talked about the Birds and the Flowers" and "there wasn't a dry Glove in the Church." "Everyone said the Sermon was Superfine and Dandy." The only thing that worried the congregation was that "to retain such a Whale it might have to Boost his Salary." Then Ade draws his moral, which is commonly to the point, "Give the people what they Think they want." "The time will come when they will not endure the sound doctrine, having itching ears, heaping to themselves teachers after their own lusts."

Higher Criticism is in line with the lusts of the modern man. Theodore Parker, the free thinker, explained his success in attracting crowds on the ground that he preached "a theology which was acceptable to human nature." That is the curse of Higher Criticism. A. J. Gordon says, "Liberalism is the religion of human nature. It does not make stern and rigid claims on men; it does not hold them up to strong convictions on such subjects as sin and retribution and the need of regeneration. Hence, when men get careless and easy-going in their opinions they drift into what is called 'liberalism' as inevitably as water runs down hill. You never find men drifting into high-Calvinism, and you never will till you find water running up hill, and iron floating upward in the air." The press has recently reported the erection of a monument in the North Benton Cemetery, Ohio. Chester Bedel, the famous infidel, who boasts that he exceeds Bob Ingersoll in his unbelief, and who is reputed to have made four trips to the Holy Land for data with which to disprove the Bible, has erected this stone. It is a representation of himself, with his foot upon the volume of the Sacred Scriptures. Few are so intense in their opposition to its holy precepts; but is not the attitude the very one occupied by many of the so-called "Critics" of the hour?

HIGHER CRITICISM AS A PROPAGANDA.

"And will turn away their ears from the truth, and be turned unto fables."

Higher Criticism makes capital of unwarranted concessions. Conservatism has unquestionably blundered. When its prophets surrendered the theory of Verbal Inspiration they discarded the very teaching of the Word itself, and unnecessarily conceded the main point in the controversy. There were many good men among us who thought to accommodate their theories of inspiration to the demands of the Critics by saying, "If God did not give the words of Scriptures, He at least inspired the thought." But Foster deserves approval for having so clearly shown that when this concession is made it is easy to force the fight to the point where no sort of inspiration remains. Manifestly, if God did not think enough of this Book to personally supervise its thought and expression, so that it would voice His mind exactly, it is hardly worth while for men to make much of it.

When Conservatives affirm that "the modern miracle is not possible" they provide Critics standing ground from which to contend against the ancient miracle; and they have made good use of it. The Bible teaches the former as clearly as the latter, and if we may not trust it in the one instance, we have no right to insist upon its claims in the other. The Conservative questions whether the sick man, who rose after prayer, was really healed of the Lord. Mr. Foster agrees with him and says, "apply your principles to ancient as well as modern times," adding, "To me it would be a hard, insufferable yoke of the letter, were I required to confess that Jesus stilled the storm on the sea with a word; or that he walked on the surface of the water without sinking." ("The Finality of the Christion Religion," p. 139.) Conservatives have talked about the evolution of a life; and keeping the children from ever going into sin, so that they would not need conversion. Critics have accepted the concession, and insisted that the old faith which regards "conversion as a miracle" "will give way to a more continual and healthy religious development, to be interpreted as 'order' and not 'miracle.'" (p. 146). Conservatives have questioned whether Christ's promise to return from heaven is to be accepted literally. Critics have taken advantage of that doubt to deny that He ever went to heaven, and scout the notion that He ever even rose from the dead. Dr. Foster declares with reference to Jesus' resurrection, "there is evidence, therefore, that it is not the soul's hope of salvation;" that it may be even "alien to the essentials of Christianity." (pp. 135-6).

If there ever was an hour in which Conservatives should see the inevitable result of compromise with doubt, and concession to unscriptural criticism, that hour is now. We have **really provided some of the seeds which they have sown in the great world-field, and for the** awful harvest of skepticism Conservatives cannot be altogether blameless.

The propaganda of Higher Criticism substitutes doubts for dogma. Christ dealt in no doubt. His apostles never framed a skeptical sentence. Higher Critics boast that they deal in "no dogma." Foster says, "We are saved by doubt as well as by faith." Surely this is "a new theology." A man doubts whether the Bible is inspired—and it helps him. He doubts whether Christ was begotten by the Holy Ghost—and it strengthens him. He doubts whether Christ ever rose from the grave—and his character is confirmed. He doubts whether Christ ever wrought a miracle—and it has a blessedly miraculous effect upon him. He doubts whether Christ ever ascended up to the right hand of God, and it lifts him nearer to that position. He doubts whether Christ ever shall return to the earth and rule from sea to sea, and it exalts him to new supremacy. "New Theology" is the name! Someone tells the story of a cat that set out to learn the secret of happiness. She met successively an ox chewing the cud, a bee gathering nectar, a bird singing to its mate, and in answer to her question how to be happy, each gave a characteristic reply. The ox bade her chew the cud; the bee, make honey; the bird, perch on a bough and sing. But as she could do none of these things she sought farther. At last she came to an owl, and he advised her to meditate. The advice seemed sensible. But what about? The owl answered "Our race has observed that the owl comes from the egg; and yet the egg comes from the owl; hence the question arises, which first existed, the owl or the egg? I ponder perpetually upon this question," said the owl. "But," returned the cat, "how are we ever to find out?" "Find out," said the owl; "we never can find out. The beauty of the question is that its solution is impossible." It remained for Higher Criticism to build its religious faith upon the same basis.

But, having found a resting place for its soul, it could not therewith be content. True meditation is almost certain to result in exploitation, and Criticism must speak. The ancient prophets and apostles taught; and Paul enjoins upon Timothy, "Do the work of an evangelist; fulfil thy ministry." The modern man must not come short in this, and so Criticism converts its opinions into a propaganda.

It provides fables for the fulfilment of one's ministry. This is the charge of the text. "They have turned aside unto fables." With fables they attempt to fulfill their ministry. To them the

Bible is "fabulous;" confessedly so. To them the superhuman birth of Christ is "fabulous." His miracles are "fabulous;" His omniscience is "fabulous;" His ascension and second coming are "fabulous;" the theory of substitution is purely so; in fact, Christ himself is fabulous. Foster dares to liken the Messiahship of Jesus Christ to the modern deception of a Santa Claus. (p. 434). This, then,, is the climax of the whole matter! Accept such a foundation for your faith if you like, "but as for me and my house, we will serve the Lord." We will accept as the foundation of our faith "The apostles and the prophets, Christ Jesus himself being the chief corner stone," and join with Theodore Cuyler in saying, "This Bible is all the dearer, not only because it has pillowed the dying heads of father and mother, but because it has been the sure guide of a hundred generations of Christians before them. When the boastful innovators offer me a new system of belief (which is really a congeries of unbelief), I say to them, 'the old is better.' Twenty centuries of experience, shared by such intellects as Augustine, Luther, Pascal, Calvin, Newton, Chalmers, Edwards, Wesley and Spurgeon, are not to be shaken by the assaults of men, who often contradict one another while contradicting God's truth."

CHAPTER VII.

SOME DEFINITIONS OF THE NEW THEOLOGY.

"And they took hold of him and brought him unto the Areopagus, saying, May we know what this new teaching is which is spoken by thee?" Acts 17:19.

It is quite impossible to pay one's respects to all Athenian theologians of the hour; and equally as needless to acquaint one's audience with all the latest philosophies of religion. When, however, a man perforce his personal ability or his important position, appears in the Areopagus of modern thought, with a novel theology, it may be worth while to ask again, "May we know what this new teaching is which is spoken by thee?"

Some time since R. J. Campbell, pastor of the City Temple, London, loomed large in the public press. This was due to the combined circumstances of personal capability and official distinction. It has been said that some of the English papers are now apologizing for having paid Mr. Campbell more attention than his mental worth warranted; but those American newspapers who had much to say concerning Prof. Geo. B. Foster, need not join their English brethren in this apology, for while Foster in "The Finality of the Christian Religion" writes in a more pompous style, and by repeated quotation and appeal conveys the impression of wider research, Mr. Campbell is his companion in the new theology, and more than his peer in original thought and felicitous expression. Like Dr. Foster he assumes to be blazing a new path for searchers after the truth; like him, also, he indulges in a philosophy of religion to the exclusion of Biblical theology; and still more like him he regards all Conservatives as out of date, and all creeds, built upon Bible statements, as obsolete. In the face of the fact that Conservatives hold the most eminent pulpits in the world, and that his great predecessor, Joseph Parker, passed away but yesterday, he unhesitatingly proclaims, "The world is not listening to theologians today; they have no message for it; they are on the periphery, not at the center of things; the great rolling river of thought and action is passing them by"—"The New Theology," page 48. This statement, of course, justifies his plea for a "new theology," and it may not be profitless to give consideration to what he has to say of such subjects as the Holy Scriptures, the God of Israel,

Jesus of Nazareth, Sin and Salvation, and the Judgment to come.

THE HOLY SCRIPTURES.

Mr. Campbell falls into the error, common to our times, of making "the place occupied by Jesus Christ the ultimate question for the Christian religion." In this mistake he has the companionship of many a Conservative. Critics have so often asserted that Christ was the starting point in our holy faith, that the more conservative brethren have grown so used to the expression as to forget that it involves a falsehood. Christ is basal in our religion; "other foundation can no man lay." But, back of foundation-laying is the work in the great quarries—the hewing of the stones! The Sacred Scriptures are the quarries of truth! Destroy them, and no Christ remains to the "modern man!" Only as you work in them does Christ come before you; only as you "handle them aright" is His character evident enough to be an inspiration. Those are intelligent people, therefore, who write down as the first article of their faith, "We believe that the Holy Bible was written by men divinely inspired, and is a perfect treasure of heavenly instruction; that it has God for its Author, salvation for its end, and truth without any mixture of error for its matter.

Therefore it is, and shall forever remain, the supreme standard by which all human conduct, creeds, and opinions, should be tried." It is little wonder that Campbell's Christ is an intellectual and moral phantom! When once a man has put dynamite into the quarries and blown them to atoms, he can not be expected to bring out of that dust-heap a great foundation stone! The best that he can do, thereafter, is stucco work, or possibly pebble dash. No one who reads after Mr. Campbell can deny that he has destroyed the quarries. In proof of this, I call your attention to his definitions of Scripture.

He rejects the authority of *the Scriptures.* He decries the tendency to bow to any external authority, whether of "church," or "statement of belief," or a supposed "infallible book" (p. 174). He affirms "the true seat of authority is within, not without the human soul." If he is right in this, every man that sails the high sea of life, is far more poorly equipped for a successful voyage, than is the modern sailor. The latter is provided, from the hydrographic office, a chart— showing the safe waters—to be studied in the darkest day and in the blackest night! But if there be no external authority in the Word of God, the immortal soul is not so equipped! It goes out to learn the truth, "little by little," as Mr.

Campbell himself expresses it, and to learn by bitter experience of mistakes, of storm, of shoals, of shipwreck. The drunken man, reeling through the streets, in his search for home, is no more uncertain in his movements than are those people who have flung away the Scripture-chart, and put their trust "in their own divine nature to enable them to follow the truth." Africans are of the same divine (?) nature as the Americans, and yet those of them who know nothing of the Word of God wander aimlessly in sin, and wallow in the sloughs, while their own black brethren who have become familiar with this Book, find it "a lamp to their feet: a light to their pathway." It is difficult to be patient with a man who is himself—in all that goes to make him civilized, in all that has effected in him any culture, in all that has created for him any Christian ideals—the product of the Bible, when one hears him asserting his independence of the very fountains of his strength. Dr. Osler's proposition to chloroform one's parents, out of whose lives he came, when they have passed fifty, is virtuous beside his behavior, who having derived his character from the Bible, turns about to deny the authority and stigmatize the teachings of the same.

Again Campbell declares *"Belief in the infallible Book is impossible"* ("The New Theology," page 178). He charges it with irreconcilable "contradictions," with "the most sanguinary exhortations;" he expresses doubt as to whether we should ever have heard of the Old Testament "if it had not been for Jesus," and defines "the New" "as only a statement of what some good men thought about Jesus and His Gospel at the beginning of Christian History" ("The New Theology," p. 178-79).

We have had many men, in modern times, who have made remarkable statements; not a few of them have been remarkable for the folly they contained, but no one of them all has ever exceeded Mr. Campbell's statement concerning the Old Testament Scriptures. The most advanced critics have conceded the antiquity of the Old Testament, and Mr. Campbell is almost the first to hint that this collection of sacred books, beginning with Genesis and ending with Malachi, received its sacred character with the coming of Jesus, or was rescued from death by his appeals to the same. On the contrary, unless one deny the veracity of the New Testament altogether, Jesus quoted from the Old because it was a sacred book, and while frankly dissenting from some of the interpreters common to His day, He fully conceded both its authority and integrity! Why else should he have answered the devil in the very language of the Old Testament, Matt. 4:7? Why should he have affirmed "Think not that I came to destroy the law of the prophets; I came not to destroy, but to fulfill; for verily I say unto you until heaven and earth shall pass away one jot or one title shall in nowise pass away from the law until all things shall be accomplished." Matt. 5: 17-18. Why should he have declared, "Whosoever therefore shall break one of these least commandments, and shall teach men so, shall be called least in the kingdom of heaven; but whosoever shall do and teach them he shall be called great in the kingdom of heaven." Matt. 5:19. But why multiply such quotations? Every man who is familiar with the Word of God knows that Jesus confirmed the utter authority of the Old Testament! To deny that is to deny Him, or else to declare that the New Testament is no trustworthy record of what He said.

Dr. Campbell concludes his discussion of the authority of the scripture in perfect accord with the custom of advanced theologians, lodging *authority in inner consciousness*—whatever that may mean. It is doubtless pleasing to the flesh to say, "we are writing a Bible with our own lives today." It is almost eloquent to affirm, "every noble life is a word of God to the world; every brave, unselfish deed is a ray of eternal truth." (p. 182). But when a man has finished that speech let it be understood that he has taken the old Book away from us, and said "look at me! God has given you no chart and compass with which to make your way over the world, but He has penned you a living epistle, and I am it,"—all of which gives point to Mr. Campbell's quotation from the witty Frenchman who said, "In the beginning God created man in His own image, and man has ever since been returning the compliment by creating God in his!" Mr. Campbell naively accepts the conclusion, saying "what else can we do?" Our answer is, "It is a poor little god New Theology has put up." If Conservatives refuse to bow before it or him, let not the critics be offended, since we decline to worship ourselves.

The dispatch with which Mr. Campbell accomplishes this disposition of the Bible, walking through the whole subject in a few minutes, giving attention to but a few texts, reminds one of nothing so much as the report of that American's visit to the British Museum. A writer says that, with the Western hustle, "he leaped out, kicked aside the pigeons that were feeding in the court, and cried to the uniformed official at the door: 'Have you still got the Elgin Marbles?' 'Yes, Sir. Of course, Sir.' 'Good! And the Assyrian winged-bulls?' 'They're still here, Sir.' 'What about those 6,000-year old human remains on the second floor—they're not sold yet, are they?' 'No, indeed, sir.' Won't you step in and see them?' 'No, thanks, I'll just take them as *per* catalogue. You see, I've got Westminister, St. Paul's, the House of Parliament and the South Kensington Museum to do this morning, and I must get a train for Oxford in time to run over the colleges before starting for Stratford for the night. So long, sir!'"

Dr. Campbell will perhaps pardon some of us if we linger longer in this court of antiquity, if we study more carefully its marble palaces, and dwell upon the symbolism of its slain calf, and listen with veneration to what its ancient prophets have spoken; pardon us, perhaps, if while we linger we think we hear God saying, "these ancient writings contain My will," and accept their promises as having a present day application to our needs, and answers to our holiest desires.

THE GOD OF ISRAEL.

With a commendable consistency Mr. Campbell rejects the God of Israel.

According to the ,'New Theology" *The Jehovah of the Old Testament was only a tribal deity.* In contending that the Semitic people belived in the community of life between the worshipper and his God, he says, "In the Semitic mind there was always a conviction that the deity of the clan, or tribe, was the giver or sustainer of its life. This did not apply to the minor divinities, demons of woods and streams, but to the tribal deities—the Chemosh of Moab, the Dagon of the Philistines, the Jehovah of Israel." Surely here is "New Theology" with a vengeance. The claims elsewhere put forth by Mr. Campbell, that the Hebrews regarded themselves as having their particular god, is out of all accord with what we find in their literature. The New Testament is not more clear in its teaching of monotheism than is the old; and, in fact, does not so often declare upon the subject of one God, and one only—the Creator and Preserver of all things—as does the Old. Even the missionary operations of the New Testament—intended to bring all men to worship this one God through His Son, Jesus Christ—are adumbrated by the work of Noah, Abraham, Joseph, Elijah, and other prophets of the true faith—that "God is one, and beside Him there is none else."

John Watson, in the "Mind of the Master," writes as truthfully as beautifully concerning the Jewish conception of "the Holy One, who was the Lord of Hosts," saying, "Jewish piety has laid the world under a hopeless debt by imagining the austere holiness of God, and has doubled the obligation by adding His tenderness. It was an achievement to carve the white marble; a greater to make it live and glow. The saints of Israel touched their highest when they infused the idea of the Divine spirituality with passion, and brought it to pass that the Holy One of Israel is the kindest deity that has ever entered the heart of man. There was no human emotion they did not assign to God; no relationship they did not use as the illustration of His love; no appeal of affection they did not place in His lips; no sorrow of which they did make Him partaker. When a prophet's inner vision has been cleansed by the last agony of pain, he dares to describe the Eternal as a fond mother who holds Ephraim by the hands, teaching him to go; who is outraged by his sin, and yet can not bear that Israel should perish: as a Husband who has offered a rejected love, and still pleads; who is stained by a wife's unfaithfulness and pursues an adulteress with entreaties. One can not lay his hand on the body of prophetical Scripture without feeling the beat of the Divine heart: one can detect in its most distant members the warmth of the Divine love." As Watson has truly taught, "faith could take but one farther step than that which it accomplished in the Old Testament: that was to see the King on the Throne, 'the Shepherd of Israel,' 'the Rock of one's individual Salvation,' 'a very present help in time of trouble,' to be a personal father;" and Jesus, who was also a Jew, taught them that; taught them, as Watson says, "That God might be a King and a Judge, but He was first of all, last of all, and through all, the Father."

Again, one is tempted to impatience when he compares the God of the Old Testament and the God of the New, with the god of Dr. Campbell's creation.

The Definition of the Doctor's god is misty, if not meaningless. He calls "it" or "him" "the uncaused cause of all existence; the uniatry principle in all multiplicity." ("The New Theology," p. 17). Again, he defines God as "the mysterious Power that is finding expression in the universe, and which is present in every atom of the wondrous whole." (p. 18).

Again and again he defines Him as "the Whole of things." This is certainly a combination of big expressions with small thinking. Some years since Thomas Dixon and Mr. Ingersoll engaged in a fiery debate, in the course of which Mr. Ingersoll charged Christianity with lack of clearness in its statement of faith, whereupon Mr.

Dixon replied by reminding the Colonel that Mr. Ingersoll's followers had started a society in New York with a Sunday evening lecture, and its leader, Mr. Frank, had at the first meeting, put forth the following clear-cut declaration of faith: "We believe in the superhuman purposive potency of Nature. We look upon the universe as the involution of the divine potentialities. The all-potential is within all and working through all. What this ultimate divine potentiality is we do not claim to be fully able to comprehend." Why Mr. Campbell went to the difficulty of another definition, when so lucid a one was extant, seems inexplicable, save on the supposition that he had not heard of this one. To a man who, like him, is tired of difficult terms and meaningless phrases, Mr. Frank's definition of faith should be a delight. In the introduction to "The New Theology," Dr. Campbell said, "I am usually able to say what I mean, and in the following pages my object is to say what I mean in such a way as everybody can understand." But after all, has the idea of God been simplified when you turn from the expression, "God is love," to the statement, "God is the un-caused cause of all existence?" Is one enlightened by leaving the sacred page, where God is presented as "Creator and upholder of all things," to listen to what Mr. Campbell has to say concerning "the mysterious Power which is finding expression in the universe?"

Again, is one rid of his difficulty when he repudiates a God who created the heavens and the earth, and is himself above them, and apart from them, as a separate entity, by accepting a God who is so identified with them that the dog is one manifestation of Him, the cat another, and even the poison-fanged serpent that crawls the earth, or the hideous monster that disports himself in the slime of the sea, a third? As between these difficulties the majority of mankind will continue to do as has been their wont, viz., adopt the old notion that "God is Creator of the heavens, yet above them," "the Maker of the earth, yet independent of it;" the Father of our spirits, yet as separate and entire, in himself, as we are from our own children. Some one has written, "He who is Christ's, surveying the wonders of Creation, can say, 'Glorious though these things be; to me belongs that which is more glorious far.' The streams are precious, but I have the Fountain; the vesture is beautiful, but the Wearer is mine; the portrait in its every lineament is lovely, but that great Original whose beauty it feebly depicts, is my own. 'God is my portion; the Lord is my inheritance.' To me belongs all actual and all possible good, all created and uncreated beauty, all that eye hath seen or imagination conceived; and more than that, for 'Eye hath not seen nor ear heard, nor hath it entered into the heart of man to conceive what God hath prepared for them that love Him. " For, over all and above all, and beyond all, is God Himself.

JESUS OF NAZARETH.

Doctor Campbell *defines Him as a man only.* To be sure, he resents this charge, and claims that "Christ is *'the only man;'* " yet his statements bind him to the proposition that Christ is a man only. He almost scoffs at the idea of His immaculate conception; He insists that infinite knowledge was not with Christ; His miracle-working he ignores; His physical resurrection he explains on the ground that there is nothing physical, save as thought takes that form. While admitting that divinity was in Jesus, he claims with equal ardor that it is in every man. He says, "God was not manifest in His flesh in any way that would cut Him off from the rest of human kind." Concerning His eternal existence, as a co-equal with the Father, he names it "a gratuitous assumption, without a shred of evidence to support it."

He admits that He was the incomparable man. In common with those who first deny His deity that they may praise His humanity, he remarks, "It is no use trying to place Jesus in a row along with other religious masters; we have no category for Him." "His influence for good is greater than all the masters of men put together, and still goes on increasing." He even admits Jesus cannot be exceeded, saying, "We have seen perfect manhood once, and that was the manhood of Jesus." Apparently he sees no inconsistency between these admissions and his theory of evolution by which he declares there has been a "gradual and unmistakable rise; the law of evolution governing in human affairs just as it does in every other cosmic process." But plain people, and some fairly well-educated and confessedly intelligent ones, will find it difficult to follow Mr. Campbell in this manipulation of notions. If evolution is true we ought to be on the whole forever ascending in the scale of human life, e'en though we suffer occasional short periods of retrogression. The man born two thousand years ago, of purely human parents, even of plain and unlearned ones, bred in the inferior schools of that time, pressed upon from every side by the ignorant prejudices of his age, should hardly prove the final product in the process of human life, the goal beyond which manhood can never go,—the climax of human character. Mr. Campbell maintains that the Old Testament never prophesied the coming of Jesus; that the promise of the Seed of woman to bruise the head of the serpent had naught to do with Him; that Isaiah's Child, to be born and to become the Wonderful, the Counsellor, the Mighty God, the Prince of Peace, the everlasting Father, pointed only to a mortal man who long since served his generation and passed away; that even the 53rd of Isaiah anticipates no suffering Messiah.

He explains Christ's death on natural grounds—it was not the fulfillment of a prophecy, but a collusion of bad men against a good one; it was not the substitution for sin, but the meaningless sacrifice of an uncompromising life; it was not the Lamb slain from the foundation of the world, but merely the vent of human hatred against holiness. How all of this comports with his theory that nothing exists outside of God; that God is in everything, and everything is only some form of divine expression, this new theologian has not told us. It is hardly to be expected that he ever will! He declares that had Jesus been gibbeted, or hung, or drowned, that his church would have made the gibbet, the rope, the water, the basis of its call, the insignia of its conquest. When one is passing through all this philosophizing about Christ he is carried along by the writer's ardor, and does not so wrathfully resent it; but when he lays aside the book, and calmly contemplates the conclusion, he is compelled to say, "not only unscriptural, but puerile," "not only irreligious, but insane." There never lived a man of sound mind, who could read the Bible through, and come to any such conclusion concerning Christ, except he had first been tutored in the school of modern skepticism, dexterously initiated into the order of the Anti-Supernaturalists. To illustrate—One day there floated into the harbor of Nagasaki a Bible. An intelligent Japanese man plucked it from the sands. Upon being told what it was, he procured a Chinese translation and began to read, and for seven years he pored over its pages. In 1866 he went to Verbeck—that remarkable man—to tell of his experience, and this is what he said: "Sir, I can not tell you my feelings, when for the first time I read the account of the character and the work of Jesus Christ. I had never seen or heard or imagined such a person. I was filled with admiration, overwhelmed with emotion, and taken captive by the record of His nature and life." It is needless to tell you that that unprejudiced Japanese believed that Jesus was the Christ prophesied in the Old Testament; born of the Virgin but begotten of the Holy Ghost; that He lived the life of spotless purity, and died the death of atoning sacrifice; that He rose literally from the grave, and in person ascended to the right hand of God, and that He there lives now to make intercession for us; that He is the actual Head of the church; the present Conqueror, and the coming King of Glory. This is the Christ of Conservatives, the Christ of the Bible, and the Christ of God. Who would exchange Him for Mr. Campbell's remarkable man, however matchless he may paint him, since it is written, "I and my Father are one!"

Having disposed of the Sacred Scriptures; the God of Israel, and the Man of Nazareth, Doctor Campbell addresses himself to

SIN AND SALVATION.

Sin he defines as only a shadow. "Evil is a negative, not a positive term; it denotes the absence rather than the presence of something; it is the perceived privation of good, the shadow where the light ought to be." "The devil," he affirms, "is a vacuum." Some of his readers will doubtless fear that an evil spirit has gotten into the Doctor's head.

Now some of us had supposed that sin denoted more than the absence of something. Drunkenness is doubtless the absence of sobriety, but is it not also the presence of spirituous liquors in possession of a man? Lust is the absence of true love, but is it not also the supremacy of evil passions? Murder is the absence of the appreciation of life, but is it not also the presence of animated destruction? Again, he defines sin as "the opposite of love;" but is it not more? Is it not the active expression of lust? So thin and shadowy is all this suggestion that Mr. Campbell himself grows tired of it. In discussing the Atonement he sanely suggests, "it is time we had done with unreal talk about sin. Sin is the murder-spirit in human experience. 'Whosoever hateth his brother is a murderer. If a man say, I love God and hateth his brother, he is a liar: for he that loveth not his brother whom he hath seen, how can he love God whom he hath not seen?' Strong language, but I suppose the man who first used it must have known what he was talking about." ("New Theology," p. 160). Did not the man who defined "sin" as "the transgression of the law, know what he was talking about? Have the judges in the civilized parts of the world had any occasion to doubt the accuracy of that definition? Has the man who visits the red-light district, or looks deeply enough into his own heart to see its recesses, ever doubted the sanity of Paul's statement of "the exceeding sinfulness of sin?" Has not Doctor Campbell himself frankly confessed his surrender to orthodoxy when he says "pomposity is sin because it is egotism; self-complacency and contemptuousness are sin for the same reason; stupidity is sin, whether in a burglar or a doctor of divinity; a bitter, grasping, cruel, unsympathetic spirit is sin, no matter who shows it." Why does not the doctor go farther and say, "the wages of sin is death;" "the soul that sinneth it shall die?" All human experiences attest that and all human observation witnesses to it.

A stranger thing than his contention that "sin is a quest for God," has never found expression in literature. His contention that the man who got drunk last night to gratify his lower nature, was mistakenly, but "really seeking God," is something new under the sun. His notion that the *roue,* who went out to destroy innocents, while in the very act of spreading death, "was seeking God," is the shrewdest definition of sin Satan has yet conceived, and the strangest definition of what God is, that any man professing to know Him has yet voiced. This opinion is changed in nothing by taking the whole context into account, except, that one is led to pity the author of such sentences, when by the context it is made evident that he is, after all, in no sympathy with sin.

It is little wonder that, with such definitions of sin, one's idea of salvation should be consequently queer. His presentation of the same is simple enough, but not so easy. He tells men to save themselves; they are their own and only saviours. Chas. Spurgeon says that he once visited Carisbrooke Castle where King Charles, of unhappy memory, had been incarcerated. His friends had planned Charles' escape; a boat was in waiting at the water's edge. Under the shadow of darkness a ladder had been put up the side of the castle, and it only remained for Charles to scale the inner walls to the window, and all the rest was easy! But alas! he had no power with which to accomplish that. The Scriptures speak of the soul as "dead in trespasses and in sin, and Mr. Campbell says, "he who is guilty of sin, is guilty of soul-murder." Query: How can the dead man save himself? When Jesus called Lazarus with a loud voice, he came forth. The day is not yet come when the dead rise without any divine assistance! That day Mr. Campbell's philosophy of salvation will be practicable, and not before!

THE JUDGMENT TO COME.

He maintains *there is none!* "There is no such thing as punishment; no far-off judgment day; no great white throne, and no judge external to ourselves." (p. 210). This is a doctrine to delight devils. It would take the fear out of their hearts. When they reflect upon the God whom they have spurned, they will cease from trembling. But all of that will not keep them from the experience appointed unto the rebels against love. To follow R. J. Campbell's speculations, when Christ has given a revelation, is not to escape judgment, but to increase it; not to fill up the lake of fire and brimstone, but to fling ourselves in as additional fuel; it is not to enter the home which God has prepared for them that love Him, but to share the fate of them who hate Him and His holy law. The most dangerous power with which any minister or even mortal man was ever possessed, is the power of mis-direction. To point people into the path that leads to the pit by persuading them that it ends in glory, is the acme of opposition to God, and the climax of service to the Adversary. For twenty centuries, yea and for thirty, men whose faces have been lit up with the light of a better world, whose feet have climbed the path "that shineth more and more to the perfect day," have walked according to the Word. The fingers of true prophets and apostles have pointed to the Celestial City, by way of the cross, and to salvation by way of the bleeding Son of God. I had rather lay down my life than hint to any man that there is "any other way given under heaven." When Sam Hadley died, one of the speakers at his funeral rehearsed the story told by William Arthur in the "Tongue of Fire" concerning one of his old friends, Robert Sutcliffe. An aged man is represented as coming to see him; they talked together, and the visitor said, "Did you know that so-and-so was dead? That this one is gone, and the other, mentioning their names," and Robert Sutcliffe answered, "So they have all gone! I suppose some of these men will meet in heaven and say, 'where is Robert Sutcliffe; he must have lost his way!'" He was still for a moment, and opening his eyes with a smile, he exclaimed, "I think not; I shall go home soon, and I can hear those aged friends of mine shouting as I climb the streets of heaven—'Here comes Robert Sutcliffe—he has not missed the way.'"

Beloved, if we accept the philosophies of men, and fling away the revelation of our God, what excuse will we be able to present for having missed the way?

Chapter VIII.

SKEPTICISM—IS SATAN BACK OF IT?

Henry Van Dyke has contributed an excellent volume entitled "The Gospel for an Age of Doubt." For the most part it is a noble defense of "the faith once delivered." In the first chapter of that volume he reminds his readers that "There is a wide-spread unsettlement of soul in regard to fundamental truths of religion, and also in regard to the nature and existence of the so-called spiritual faculties by which alone thes truths can be perceived. In its popular manifestations, this unsettlement takes the form of uncertainty rather than of denial, of unbelief rather than of disbelief, of general skepticism rather than of specific infidelity. The questioning spirit is abroad, moving on the face of the waters, seeking rest and finding none. The age stands in doubt."

The so-called Advanced Thinkers, occupying some of our pulpits, seem to suppose that the Gospel for such an Age should itself be "uncertain." Many of them, refusing to favor homeopathy in medicine, have, nevertheless, carried its tocsin, "Similis curantur similibus" to the utmost extent in theology, and propose to save a doubting world by dosing it with additional doubt, and we are even told now that "Doubt is no sin." And, whereas the Bible tells us we are "saved by faith" and "sanctified by truth," these self-styled "Thinkers" actually affirm "We are saved by doubt" and "sanctified by skepticism."

In discussing the subject, "Doubt—Is the Devil Back of It?" we want to take our position beside Christ and listen to His definitions of doubt, watch Him when He is dealing with doubt, and hear what He has to say on the subject of redemption from doubt, for, with a strange inconsistency, the majority of the Critics, while denying the integrity of the Word, are still trying to cling to the authority of Christ.

THE DEFINITION OF DOUBT.

If one is to accept even the Standard Dictionary: "Doubt is to hesitate to accept as true or certain." "To be skeptical concerning!" "To hold to be questionable or uncertain! To distrust!"

Christ met men who maintained toward Him, toward His work and toward His Word, doubt. These men were at that time naturally divided into three classes, and the same divisions obtain to this minute, viz., the uninstructed, the non-convinced and the indisposed.

The uninstructed! Ignorance has always and everywhere been the basis of much doubt. We have a phrase that "Ignorance is the mother of credulity." It is none the less the mother of incredulity. You tell the ignorant man about the infinity of space and instantly he takes on a quizzical smile. You tell the ignorant man about the multitude of worlds and the relative littleness of the earth, and his look as perfectly phrases "Why don't you quit lying?" as if he voiced it. He may be the recipient of all the blessings incident to the Divine arrangement of the universe, and yet see God in none of it, solely because he is uninstructed. In the ninth chapter of John's Gospel we have recorded one of the most remarkable miracles known to the New Testament. A man, blind from his birth, is instantly given his sight. They asked him concerning his healer, "Where is he?" He answered, "I do not know." They asked him, "Who is he?" He answered, "I do not know." They asked him, "How did he do it?" He answered, "I do not know." They said, "The man who healed you is a sinner." He answered, "Whether he is a sinner I know not; one thing I know, that whereas I was blind I now see." The man's unbelief in the diety of Jesus Christ was a pure result of his ignorance of Him. When Jesus returned to him and asked him, "Dost thou believe on the Son of God?" he was compelled to answer, "Who is he, Lord, that I might believe on Him?" We are not ready to say that this man was responsible for his ignorance. A blind man has not the opportunity of knowedge accorded to others. Nor would we characterize him as a "sinner" because of his doubt. But when the time came that the Lord returned and stood before his open vision, and said unto him, "Thou hast both seen him, and it is He that speaketh with thee" had he not then fallen down to worship Him, his continued skepticism would have been Satan's triumph.

An impression exists in some quarters to the effect that men are being made skeptical in this country by their increasing knowledge. On the contrary they are being made skeptical by their increasing ignorance! The children of this generation may know five times as much Science as did their fathers and mothers; they do not know one-tenth as much Scripture! They talk of "the assured results of scientific investigation" because they have followed that far enough to feel that it is true; and they talk about the "errancy of the Scriptures" because they have so grossly neglected them that they do not know their content. This neglect is not a necessity;

hence it is sin. How then, can the skepticism born of it be less than sin?

The non-convinced! There are skeptical men and women who are not chargeable with ignorance of Scriptural things, but who are either from Ireland or Missouri. The Irishman said, "I am open to conviction, but I would like to see the man that will convince me!" And the Missourian said, "You'll have to show me!"

For the present we want to deal with the latter, and, without discussion, admit that he may be a perfectly honest doubter. There are such men and there are such women. They have studied the Scripture some; they have studied skeptical men more. The latter have filled them with interrogation points. It is natural that these men and women should be found in the student body. When Henry Drummond said, "Some of the finest young fellows with whom I am acquainted, university men, are among the most skeptical," he said the true thing. Why should it not be so? The average man or woman who enters the schools has never even read the Bible from cover to cover. He has dipped in here and dipped in there, and his knowledge is neither extensive, intensive, nor systematized. The very methods employed in the school have been ignored in his Biblical training. Great sections of the Word, he has never seen. At the average school there is no arrangement whatever to make him familiar with it; and in some schools the very men appointed to instruct him in the same talk learnedly of the "literary value of the Bible" and reveal at the same time their utter indifference to its divine character, and its spiritual import. Think of a freshman in an Indiana college, assigned the book of Job as the subject of his essay, putting in at the library to ask for the same, and expressing his surprise to discover that it was in the Bible. Think of 96 men in the Northwestern University—a hot-bed of skepticism—questioned as to what the Penteteuch was, and 30 of them unable to answer; asked where the book of Jude was, and 40 of them unable to tell that it was in the New Testament; asked to mention one of the judges, and 51 failing; asked to name three kings of Israel, and 49 giving it up; asked to name three prophets, and 44 confessing their inability. Twenty of those students could not write a single Beatitude. And 65 of the 96 could not quote one verse from the epistle to the Romans. For Judges they named Solomon, Nehemiah, Daniel and Lazarus. For the prophets they named Matthew, Luke, Herod and Ananias. It is such students who enter a professor's chair later in life, and go Ingersoll one better. Bob Ingersoll, blatant as he was in his infidelity, never denied the immortality of the soul. Shortly before his death he wrote a little poem which runs after this manner:

> "Is there, beyond the silent night
>   An endless day?
> Is death a door that leads to light?
>   We may not say.
> The tongueless secret hid in fate
>   We may not know:
> We hope and wait."

It takes a professor in our own University—Minnesota—where doubt is glorified by some as an evidence of intellectual superiority—to be dead certain that "there is no immortality of the soul," and to laugh the Scripture-teaching out of court.

The Indisposed! No man can honestly study the skepticism of the present day and escape the conviction that a vast deal of it is a result neither of ignorance of the Scripture, nor a lack of overwhelming argument in favor of its inspiration, but it is rather an indisposition. The ninth chapter of John's Gospel deals with this class also. When the Pharisees had been instructed by the man to whom vision was given as to now he got his sight; when he himself stood before them, an undisputable evidence of the truth of his words, they resorted to the exact phrase of modern skeptics, and discredited his standing, saying, "Thou wast born in sin, and dost thou teach us? And they cast him out." Jesus immediately appeared upon the scene and said, "For judgment come I into this world, that they that see not may see; and that they that see may become blind." The Pharisees appreciated the point of His speech, and said, "Are we also blind?" to which Jesus made the remarkable answer, "If ye were blind ye would have no sin; but now ye say, We see; therefore your sin remaineth." In other words, your skepticism is the pure product of a personal conceit; and your infidelity is the fruit of the indisposition to be convinced.

Joseph Parker never did a better job of riddling skepticism than when he answered Mr. Horton's series of "Tentative Suggestions" with the volume, "None Like It—A Plea for the Old Sword." London's great preacher says, with some degree of sarcasm, and yet with perfect occasion, "Unbelief is not confined to technicalities. It is really a mistake to suppose that Unbelief is standing outside the ring-fence of Faith, sobbing out its tender heart and begging Christian scholars to explain how, in Samuel, David took from the King of Zobah a thousand and seven hundred horsemen; and how, in Chronicles he took from the same king, apparently on the same occasion, a thousand chariots and seven thousand horsemen. Dear, sweet, guileless Unbelief is quite prepared to enter the church and enjoy the sacraments, if only the number of horses could be made the same in one book as it is in the other. No, no; that is not the measure of Unbelief. That is only where Unbelief begins! When he has been satisfied respecting the horse and his rider, the docile Infidel will say, 'And how are the dead raised up, and with what body do they come?' Do not imagine that the delightful Infidel, that pet of all juveniles, is only waiting to see the Hexateuch properly dated, and properly signed, in order that he may adopt the creeds and idolize 'the historic episcopate.' Infidelity, where it is honest and courageous, sets its face against the whole line of the supernatural, the revealed and the inspired, and not merely against certain literal and obvious discrepancies. By all means let discrepancies be reconciled or removed —scholarship is quite equal to this useful work— but do not suppose that the successful readjustment of chronologies, dates, and authorships will lead the Infidel to accept the Bible as 'the inspired record of the Word of God.' I question whether it would even help him to do so. Possibly it would bring into more vivid and revolting significance the fact that he 'did not like to retain God in his knowledge' " (Rom. 1:28).

Men sometimes talk as if skepticism were only a difference of thinking and that one man is as much entitled to his opinion as the other But is it not also a difference of living? We hold to utter freedom of thought. It is the privilege of any man in the world to think as he pleases. But it is not the special privilege of any soul on earth to escape the consequences of his thinking. If he think crookedly, he will produce a harvest of crime. If he think falsely and one believes him he will behave after the same manner. If he think God out of his universe, the devil will reign in him without a rival. You tell us, then. it is no sin to doubt the great verities that provide the only foundation for righteousness? In France only a little more than a hundred years ago they were spending $450,000,000 a year in printing and distributing skeptical literature. What was the result? The Bible was discredited, God was denied, the Sabbath was abolished, the church was paralized in its every part, and, as a magazine puts its, "Hell broke loose; one half the children born in Paris were bastards. 1,022,351 persons were beheaded, shot, drowned, outraged, and done to death between September, 1792, and December, 1795. Even today about one-third of the births in Paris are illegitimate. 10,000 new born are fished out of the city sewers in a single year. The Republic lives in the throes of its former infidelity." Its population is decreasing. Its suicides multiply. "Who says skepticism is not a sin?" "By their fruits ye shall know them." That phrase contains the most relentless logic that was ever thrown into human speech.

It is very beautiful to get around you a company of young men and women who have very little knowledge of what you are talking about, and spin your theories, and set yourself up as an advanced thinker! But who is going to reap the harvest? Who is going to hold his position when the whirlwind comes? If we were asked what was the basal factor in the world's skepticism, we should answer in one word—"*sin!*" If we were asked who was the chief author of the world's infidelity, we should answer in one word—"Satan!"

DEALING WITH DOUBT.

Come now to a study of Christ's dealing with doubt. Let us see how He behaved toward it.

When genuine, Christ graciously condoned it. Peter once doubted his Lord's ability, and the sea opened beneath his feet and he began to sink. Jesus did not say, "Let him go; he is only a skeptic anyhow." But the moment Peter cried for help, He stretched forth His hand and lifted him up. Thomas doubted the resurrection of Christ and declared he would never believe it until it was demonstrated to his physical senses. Thomas was quite a *"scientist,"* we would have you understand! And Jesus regarded that fact, but finding him a sincere scientist, he made the revelation. A leper doubted the disposition of Christ and approached him, saying, "Lord, if thou wilt, thou canst make me clean." Jesus did not condemn him, but said, "I will, be thou clean," because down in the heart of the doubter was a sincere desire and a struggling hope. The epileptic's father doubted the power of Christ. He said, "Lord, if thou canst do anything, have mercy upon us and help us." Jesus did not condemn him; he condoned the offense and instructed him. "If thou canst believe, all things are possible to him that believeth," and He healed his child. Campbell Morgan, referring to these incidents, said, "Do you see that these men were not certain, but in their skepticism they ventured on Christ." One came to him on a crutch because he could not walk straight. And the crutch was a little "if." "Lord, if thou wilt." And the other had to get a little crutch—a crutch for the other side. He said, "If thou canst, do something for my boy." And how did the Master deal with him? Did He say, "No, you are an unbeliever?" Never! If a man got to Him, Christ did not care how he came. It is better to know, and to say, "Lord, thou canst! I believe!" But if you cannot come that way, come with your "if." Only, come! The genuine skeptic will be received. His doubts will be dispelled! His difficulties will be abolished! His sore will be healed!

When superficial, Christ skillfully uncovered it. We shall never forget a time when Dr. James Peter Boyce, one of the most splendid and perfect gentlemen and one of the most superb scholars America ever produced, sat in his chair teaching "Systematic Theology." It was one of those days when he let the class run wild a bit, and the boys poured in a volley of questions, and did the cute student trick of making the old man recite, and they thus escape recitation. He answered them as they came, presenting his Scripture in defense of his positions, easily parrying their thrusts. Finally a Mexican from the rear of the room, his face all aglow, shouted out, "Ah, Doctor, they can't catch you!"

But the one crowd who found themselves face to face with a man who could not be caught with their captious questions was the crowd that came up against the Christ; it is interesting to note the way He answered one such company. And mark you, they were Sadducees—they were the advanced thinkers of His day. They were "the Liberal" company of Israel. They were the "Scientists" who denied the possibility of a miracle, and stood for the uniformity of natural law and for evolution. So they said, making their attack upon Moses, who to this moment is the subject of their attacks, "Moses said, If a man die, having no children, his brother shall marry his wife, and raise up seed unto his brother. Now there were with us seven brethren: and the first, when he had married a wife, deceased, and, having no issue, left his wife unto his brother: likewise the second also, and the third, unto the seventh. And last of all the woman died also. Therefore in the resurrection whose wife shall she be of the seven, for they all had her?" Now mark the answer, "Jesus answered and said unto them. Ye do err, not knowing the scriptures, nor the power of God." And then to prove that they had no knowledge of the Scriptures, He went on and rehearsed in their hearing what the Scriptures taught concerning the resurrection.

If the skeptics of this country should set themselves to a serious study of the

Word of God, and be willing to come into a personal experience of the power of God, they would not only be silenced, as were these Sadducees, but they could even be saved, for we are saved and set free by the knowledge of the truth. A little while ago, in the city of Chicago, a widely known skeptic went into the Ministers' meeting on a Monday morning when Dr. James Orr, of Scotland, that great scientist and stalwart defender of the faith, was to speak, and before he had finished with that infidel's ideas and plagiaristic customs, the latter slunk from the room, perhaps as much ashamed of the weakness of his late volume as he was over the fact which Orr brought out that he had filched pages from a German author, using them as his own, without so much as a hint that they were the product of another mind.

When insincere, Christ severely excoriated it. He charged Saduccees and Pharisees with insincerity in their skepticism toward Him. And then He called them "hypocrites," "whitened sepulchers," "viperous brood." Evidently the rejection of the deity of Jesus was no light matter in the mind of our Master. Evidently the rejection of the Word of God was, in His judgment, nothing short of wickedness. He affirmed that the unbelieving were under condemnation. He declared, that he that rejected Him rejected God, and that he that refused to hear His word would fall before the inexorable judgment of the same. Think you that Jesus did this because of personal pique? Never! He did it because he knew the fruits of infidelity. He knew that it was so, as Charles Kingsley makes Raphael Aben-Ezra, to say to Hypatia—the brilliant, superficial skeptic, who was willing to fling away all revelation that she might follow out her fine-spun philosophies— "Hypatia, I am older than you—wiser than you, if wisdom be the fruit of the tree of knowledge. You know but one side of the medal, (skepticism) Hypatia, and the fairer; I have seen its reverse form of human thought, of human action, of human sin and folly, I have been wandering for years, and found no rest—as little in wisdom as in folly, in spiritual dreams as in sensual brutality. I could not rest in your Platonism—I will tell you why hereafter. I went on to Stoicism, Epicurism, Cynicism, Skepticism, and in that lowest depth I found a lower depth, when I became skeptical of skepticism itself."

"There is a lower depth still," thought Hypatia to herself, as she recollected last night's magic; but she did not speak. What was the magic of last night? Sin! The very thing to which Raphael had himself been led, until he says, "I was on a level with my dog—the poor, dumb brute—yea, lower, for she obeyed the laws God had appointed for her control, while I broke them, everyone." When did doubt ever bring men to do less? When did skepticism ever make a saint?

Dr. Reuben A. Torrey, at the close of a sermon on "Unbelief" said, "I want to ask every man who has been saved from intemperance, or other sin, by faith in Christ and the Bible, to stand up." Something like a thousand men rose to their feet. Then, continuing, he said, "Now I want to be fair! I want any unbeliever who has been saved from his intemperance or other sin, by his infidelity, to stand." The preacher looked, not expecting any one to stand. But far back under the gallery, a man was struggling to his feet. Dr. Torrey said, "Stand up and tell it out, my man; how did your unbelief save you?" But the man beside him said, "He can't tell it; he's drunk!"

REDEMPTION FROM DOUBT.

Did Christ have an antidote for doubt? "If any man willeth to do his will, he shall know of the teaching, whether it be of God."

"If any man willeth!" Willingness ought to be a product of thought. No man will ever be redeemed from doubt unless he thinks. And it cannot be flippant thinking; it cannot be superficial philosophising. It ought to be deep and profound and continued thought. David said, "I thought on my ways, and turned my feet unto thy testimonies; I made haste and delayed not to keep thy commandments." The skeptics are very fond of the phrase, "The thinking man believes" so and so. But if experience is to be our guide, the man who truly thinks, and thinks truly, at one and the same time, can not remain skeptical.

Redemption from doubt comes by way of an inquiring mind. Nicodemus did not know whether Jesus was the Christ. He made up his mind to find out. He went into His presence. He put to Him his troublesome questions. He came away from Him convinced. The Rich Young Ruler did not know the way of life. He ran after the Lord, and falling at His feet, made inquiry. Even though he did not do what Jesus said, he went from His presence convinced. How can a man think, and yet at the same time believe that this universe is not the product of an Infinite Person, possessed of an Infinite mind? How men can prate their infidelity, when apart from faith we can do nothing, it is difficut to understand.

"Whoever plants a seed beneath the sod
And waits to see it push away the clod,
    He trusts in God.

Whoever sees 'neath winter's wealth of snow
The silent harvest of the future grow,
    God's power doth know.

Whoever says when clouds are in the sky—
'Be patient, heart, Light cometh by and by,'
    Trusts the Most High.

Whoever lies down on his couch to sleep
And locks his sense in slumber deep,
    Knows God will keep.

Whoever says 'tomorrow' the unknown,
The future, trusts the Power alone
    He dares disown.

Whoever sees in death the eyelids close,
And yet can live when life has only woes,
    God's comfort knows."

Redemption from doubt is accomplished by a responsive heart. A man's intellectual difficulties may be solved and yet he may not be saved. It was so with the Scribes, and, beyond doubt, with Felix, also. The questions were answered, but the heart was still held by sin. There is a point at which questions should cease, and worship should commence. As some one has said, "When God called to Moses to stop; to come no nearer the burning bush, it was an indication that inquiry was to cease, and worship was to begin." That is the point at which our thinking has arrived. We have glorified "investigation" and despised "devotion." We have proposed to submit everything to the microscope and the scalpel, and if we cannot find the soul, to deny it; and if with natural vision we can not see God, to decry Him. For Moses to have walked up to the bush would have been to find no fire; or else to have died there by disregarding, at one and the same time his sinful condition, and God's uncompromising holiness. "With the heart man believeth unto righteousness." When the intellect is convinced, let the knees bend; let the face go to the dust, and God will speak and in the sound of His voice the soul will lose forever its skepticism.

The redemption from doubt is best assured by an obedient spirit. Saul was not a doubter; he was a disbeliever! He disregarded the claims of Christ. He denied the authority of His Word. He derided the thought of His deity. But when overwhelmed and convinced, he cried, "Lord, what wilt thou have me to do?" And from that point, until the day when they led him out to his martyrdom, he never had a doubt. When the spirit of obedience came in, the spirit of skepticism found no room. "If any man is willing to do His will he shall *know.*" The way before him may not be fully lighted, but at its darkest passage he will feel the guiding Hand.

A young woman says, "I went through the Cave of the Winds at Niagara. The path was narrow, the sound of the falling water drowned every other sound. The spray blinded me and I could not see where I was going. I seemed to be deaf, and blind. But I clung to a strong, steady hand, and did not really feel afraid. The guide held me and drew me forward, and I had nothing to do but follow, until by and by we were in the clear shining again."

We see the way! Shall we not walk in it—inspired by His willingness and power to bring us safely home?

Chapter IX.

SCIENTIFIC SPIRIT IN SCRIPTURE STUDY.

"Give diligence to present thyself approved unto God, a workman that needeth not to be ashamed, handling aright the word of truth. But shun profane babblings: for they will proceed further in ungodliness, and their word will eat as doth a gangrene: of whom is Hymenaeus and Philetus; men who concerning the truth have erred, saying that the resurrection is past already, and overthrown the faith of some. Howbeit the firm foundation of God standeth, having this seal, the Lord knoweth them that are his: and, Let every one that nameth the name of the Lord depart from unrighteousness." (2 Tim. 2:15-19.)

The most ardent opponent of the so-called "New Theology" is not a conservative "Modern" but a progressive "Ancient." In Germany, Bettex is looked upon by Liberals as a most ardent opponent of their opinions; in France the scholarly Gaussen was feared, and with good reason, by the professed Progressives; in Scotland today James Orr stands like a granite shore-line to resist the rising tide of skepticism; in England such men as Spurgeon, Parker, Meyer and Morgan have made the endeavors of so-called progressive pulpits appear almost pitiful; while in America, the names of the truly noble who have not become enamored of Athenian theology, but who have answered every Critic so eloquently as to exasperate him, are too numerous to mention.

And yet, towering above any one of them, and all of them, as an opponent of so-called "New Theology," is a man who was put to death two thousand years ago for the faith that was in him, but who "though dead, yet speaketh," and from whose pen we take our text—even Paul. It is little wonder that the Athenian theologians have asserted that he was not inspired and have sought to discredit him, since his writing anticipated them with an eloquence that is commanding, and a logic that is relentless. If one deny the inspiration of the Apostle he is yet compelled to attend upon what he says. So colossal a figure cannot be counted out when subjects to which he addressed himself are under discussion; and, certainly he wrote concerning the scientific spirit in Scripture study.

What are the suggestions of this text? Four at least, with their subdivisions: The Scientific

Spirit; The Inspired Scriptures; The Skeptical Professor, and The Philosophy of the Steadfast.

THE SCIENTIFIC SPIRIT.

Paul was no poor student! Never once did he set his approval upon ignorance, lack of study or research. The language of this text is a revelation of the Apostle's character and customs. "Give diligence to present thyself approved unto God, a workman that needeth not to be ashamed, handling aright the word of truth." That is the scientific spirit.

The scientific spirit manifests itself in diligent research.. "The Biblical World" for August, 1908, says, "The time has come when the scientific spirit must be adopted in Bible study." Who objects? Who ever did object; and when? The point of controversy between Progressives and Conservatives is not a question as between the scientific and the unscientific spirit. Every intelligent Conservative believes in the research that is scientific. And, well equipped Conservatives are quite as capable of determining what is scientific as are Liberals. It is a singular circumstance when a man like R. J. Campbell, better known because he is the successor to the conservative Joseph Parker than for all other reasons combined, prates about the "conclusions of science" and talks as if he was an expert in the whole realm, when the truth is that his educational advantages were comparatively slight, and his theological studies were received from no school whatever. Other men, like Mr. Spurgeon and Campbell Morgan, not having enjoyed a theological seminary course, were Spirit-taught, which is even better; but Mr. Campbell seems to have been self-taught. The scientists never had a chance at him in the student days; and as for the Spirit, he repudiates His instruction. And yet, being a Liberal, there is a wide-spread opinion that he is learned. Alas for the conceit that "skepticism" and "smartness" are synonymous! It was of that very thing the Apostle wrote when he said concerning some, "who, knowing God, glorified him not as God, but became vain in their reasoning, and professing themselves to be wise, they became fools; and exchanged the truth of God for a lie, and worshipped and served the creature rather than the Creator." (Rom. 1: 21, 22, 25).

The great scientists of the past have, with wonderful unanimity, believed the Bible, and neither Faraday, Kepler, nor Newton ever felt that they had to surrender "the scientifiic spirit" in order to accept Scripture conclusions, while Lord Kelvin, who, from the early age of twenty-two, at which time he became Professor of Natural Philosophy in Glasgow University, down to the ripened period of 83—or 61 years—brought his scientific mind to bear upon the inspired Book and never found occasion to cast any part of it away, or call into question its utter authority. Not many in America but know something of the scientific accomplishments and professional skill of Dr. Howard A. Kelley, of Baltimore. He has recently contributed an article to Appleton's Magazine entitled "Out of Uncertainty and Doubt into Faith," the purpose of which was to show that when he brought his well-trained mind and an open heart to the study of the Bible, he was not only convinced that it was inspired, but compelled to accept every one of its great doctrines, approve its plan of salvation, and yield his intellect and will to the authority of its commands. He says, "I found that the Bible claimed to be the authoritative Word of God, and by taking it as my text-book of religion, testing it by submitting to its conditions, I came to believe the Book the inspired Word of God; inspired in a sense utterly different from that of any merely human book." "I believe Jesus Christ to be the Son of God, without human father, conceived by the Holy Ghost, born of the Virgin Mary; that all men, without exception, are by nature sinners, alienated from God, and when thus utterly lost in sin, the Son of God himself came down to earth, and by shedding his blood upon the cross, paid the infinite penalty of the guilt of the whole world. I believe he who thus receives Jesus Christ as his Saviour, is born again spiritually as definitely as in his first birth, and, so born spiritually, has new privileges, appetites and affections; that he is one body with Christ the Head and will live with him forever. I believe no man can be saved by what is known as a 'moral life,' such works being but the necessary fruits and evidence of the faith within." And Kelley concludes, "If faith so reveals God to me, I go without question wherever He may lead me. I can put His assertions and commands above every seeming probability in life, dismissing cherished convictions and looking upon the wisdom and ratiocinations of men as folly if opposed to Him. I place no limits to faith when once vested in God, the sum of all wisdom and knowledge, and can trust Him though I should have to stand alone before the world declaring Him to be true."

Who are these that are boasting their scientific ability, and insinuating that the Scriptures are to go down before it? Had they lighted their little candles from Kelvin's torch they might live their lives in greater light, and certainly would have less to say concerning "the conflict of science and the Scriptures." Had they given one-half as much time to the earnest study of science as has Howard A. Kelley, and like him, turned from the study of God's revelation in the physical world to a careful and prayerful perusal of the Sacred Scriptures, they might have come to the same conclusions. Let us have a scientific spirit; but let it be the spirit of science and not the spirit of shallowness.

The scientific spirit will concern itself with the Divine approval. As some has put it, "So far as a man is at all scientific he is thinking God's thoughts after Him." And the true Christian will be vastly concerned to so think as to meet the Divine approval. We are told that Da Vinci's first great endeavor to produce a work of art resulted solely from the desire to please his studio master, and that when the great teacher came and looked upon it, it was so surpassingly beautiful that he looked upon the lad and said, "I shall never paint again." The truth is that our God has deliberately decided to paint no more pictures of revelation, and to write no more His revealed will; but he lays it upon us to incarnate His conceptions and translate His revelations, that the world shall see His work in us. A true student, therefore, can but desire to secure the Divine approval upon his research.

The scientific spirit will be careful in the use of the Divine Word. The discoveries of today always demand the preservation and propagation of yesterday's knowledge. The man who proposes, therefore, to begin the study of the Bible by despising the conclusions of his fathers, may be regarded as an iconoclast, but can hardly be considered a scientist. This is not the morning of scientific research! The day of scientific discovery is well advanced! We are not emerging out of darkness that makes every vision new, and every treatise original. We have to give consideration to what our fathers thought, and attend upon what our teachers have said. The Bible has been too long in use for people to talk as if none of its tenets were true. The youth of this country, listening to the talk of present-day Critics, have been brought to think that the Koran, the Eddas of the Scandinavians, the Tribitaka of the Buddhist, the Five Kings of China, the three Vedas of the Hindoos and the Zend Avesta, are all as ancient as the Scriptures, if not more so. Well-instructed men know this is false. The Scandinavian Eddas are 1400 years younger than the latest Scripture; the Koran 700; the Buddist revelation, while it antedates Christ, could easily have borrowed its best parts from the Sacred Books of the Old Testament. Practically every one of them was written before it came into existence; while much of that Old Testament antedates the so-called revelations of China, of India, and of Persia. Its very age, therefore, demands a reverential use; while its accomplishments command and compel its sacred study.

He who professes to study light, scientifically, will be compelled to take the sun into account; and the man who proposes to introduce the scientific spirit into the study of religion will be equally compelled to consider the moral luminary of the universe, the Book of books, known throughout the world as "The Bible." By all means let us be scientific!

THE INSPIRED SCRIPTURES.

What does the Apostle mean by his phrase, "The Word of Truth?" Jesus had already spoken to this theme, praying to His Father to sanctify his disciples "through the truth," and adding "Thy word is truth." Paul, writing to the Ephesians of "the hope we have in Christ in whom ye believe" says, "having heard the word of truth—the gospel of your salvation." Unquestionably James was speaking of that part of the Bible with which he was familiar, when he declared that God "of his own will brought us forth by the word of truth." The very language employed involves the doctrine of inspiration, the necessity of illumination and the truth of Spirit-instruction.

Inspiration alone can insure the truth. The reason the writings of the most scientific men the world has known go out of date and pass away, is because their successors discover error in their conclusions. The most scientific spirit does not insure unchangeable conclusions; inspiration alone can do that. If you are going to have a Gospel that will forever remain "profitable for doctrine, for reproof, for correction, and for instruction in righteousness," it must be inspired. No fault must be found in it. The reason Harvey's discovery of the circulatory system will remain forever a fact, is not because Harvey said it, but because when Moses wrote "The life is in the blood" he voiced what was intrinsically true. The reason why the law of gravity will have to be regarded by all great scientists, is not because Newton affirmed it to be a fact. Newton sometimes made mistakes, but because God himself bethought and spoke it, as Job long since wrote, "He hangeth the world on nothing." The reason why our modern scientists are eschewing certain animals as unfit to eat and favoring others, is not because of physicians only (they are too often in error), but because when Moses wrote the Book of Leviticus he was so perfectly inspired as to make no mistake as to what was under the ban and what in favor from the standpoint of human health. Science reaches accuracy only after a thousand experiments, and climbs into the light only after a long journey out of enveloping darkness; but inspiration speaks once and it "standeth fast." It turns its face to the rising sun and wears light as a garment! Of no other book written in the world can it be said, as Christ has already affirmed concerning the Bible, "Thy word is truth."

And yet, *illumination is essential to the understanding of the Scriptures.* "The natural man receiveth not the things of the Spirit of God, neither indeed can he know them, because they are spiritually discerned. Beecher was right when he said, "The Bible will not give up its secrets to those who approach it with their bellowing passions and perverted intentions."

Huxley was supposed to be a great scientist, but confessed that that part of his nature which might have enjoyed painting or music was atrophied. Does any man mean to suggest that the carnal man may not be so thoroughly lacking in all religious intuitions as to make the meaning of revelation to him impossible? When Abraham Lincoln, the great President, was visiting in the Soldiers Home, Joshua F. Speed, his intimate friend, came to the Home to spend the night with him. Rising just after sunrise he ran up to the President's room. He found him reading a book. Looking over his shoulder he found it was the Bible. Jocularly, Mr. Speed said, "I am glad to see you so profitably employed!" "Yes," answered the great Lincoln; "I am profitably employed!" Well," said Speed, "I wonder if you have recovered from that skepticism that once characterized you. I confess frankly that I have not." Lincoln looked into his face for a moment, and then rising, put his hand on his shoulder and tenderly said, "You are wrong, Speed! Take all of this Book upon reason that you can and the rest on faith, and you will, I am sure, live, and die a better and a happier man." But whether one receives it on reason or on faith, if he is to understand it, the Spirit must instruct him and he must bring to that holy instruction a teachable spirit. Of the office of the Holy Ghost, Christ himself said, "When he is come he will guide you into all truth." He cannot guide a man who rejects Him; nor yet the man who refuses Jesus as **Teacher, for of Him** again it is said, "He shall not speak of himself; he shall take of the things of Christ and show them unto you."

THE SKEPTICAL PROFESSOR.

Here is Paul's description of him: "Shun profane babblings: for they will proceed further in ungodliness, and their word will eat as doth a gangrene: of whom is Hymenaeus and Philetus; men who concerning the truth have erred, saying that the resurrection is past already, and overthrown the faith of some." What about the skeptical Professor? Three things!

First, *he has erred concerning the truth*. Paul says, in illustration of his charge he has denied "the resurrection." That is definite and marvelously up to date. George Burman Foster denies the resurrection; R. J. Campbell denies the resurrection. Prof. Willets, in a recent article, does not deny the resurrection, but does doubt the immaculate conception. John is as much inspired as Paul, and John says, "Who is a liar but he that denieth that Jesus is the Christ?" (1 Jno. 2:22). Concerning the immaculate conception it is written "That which is conceived in her is of the Holy Spirit." To deny that is to face another indictment from the pen of the Apostle John, "He that believeth not God hath made him a liar; because he hath not believed in the witness that

God hath borne concerning his Son." (1 Jno. 5:10). In talking some time since with a Conservative minister concerning certain utterances by Prof. Willetts, of which excerpts had appeared in the papers, he said, "I am glad to see that he does not deny the resurrection of Jesus." But is not the denial of the immaculate conception equally infidel with the denial of the resurrection? and either of them puts a man outside the pale of evangelical fellowship.

Again, *the skeptical Professor has overthrown the faith of his fellows.* The word is, "Men who concerning the truth have erred, saying that the resurrection is past already, and overthrown the faith of some." How often that thing has occurred, who can tell? Not a few times in recent years have we had young men confess to us that in the course of their studies they had lost their faith in Christ as God, and the Bible as the Word of God. One of these, said, "I would give the world to believe in the Bible as you seem to do." It is a terrific arraignment Jesus Christ brings against those who destroy the faith of their fellows, "Whoso shall cause one of these little ones that believe on me to stumble, it is profiitable for him that a great millstone should be hanged about his neck, and that he should be sunk in the depth of the sea. Woe unto the world because of occasions of stumbling! for it must needs be that the occasions come, but woe to that man thro whom the occasion cometh." Walter Scott writes regarding the Bible:

> "Within this simple volume lies
> The mystery of mysteries!
> Happiest they of human race
> To whom God has given grace
> To read, to fear, to hope, to pray,
> To lift the latch, to force the way.
> And better had they ne'er been born
> Who read to doubt, or read to scorn."

It is the boast of Higher Critics that they are building men up in the faith, increasing their confidence in the Word, and so on. Where? When? Who? It is said there was a lawyer in the early days of the Indian Territory, named Mullins, who practiced in the minor courts and who made a great reputation for his ornate language. He was engaged in defending a man charged with hog-stealing one day, and, when it came time to sum up, he arose and assumed a portentous attitude before the jury: "If your Honor please," he said, "and gentlemen of the jury: I would not, for a moment, mutilate the majesty of the law nor contravene the avoirdupois of the testimony. But, and I speak advisedly, I want you homogeneous men on the jury to focalize your five senses on the proposition I am about to present to you. 'In all criminal cases there are three essential elements: the *locus in quo,* the *modus operandi* and the *corpus delicti.* In this case I think I am safe in saying the *corpus delicti* and the *modus operandi* are all right, but, gentlemen, there is an entire absence of the *locus in quo.*" That is the difficulty with Higher Criticism. Where and when did they ever do less than destroy the faith of their fellows? Look at Germany! It is an answer to my question. Look at Scotland! You will see the question being answered at this moment. Even godless Goethe was wiser than the followers of his own philosophy, for he said, "If you have convictions, give them to me; if you have doubts, keep them to yourself; I have doubts enough of my own."

He has cleared the path for moral perversion. "Shun profane babblings: for they will proceed further in ungodliness, and their word will eat as doth gangrene." One of the most definite reasons for the prevalence of present-day gilded vice is in the loss of faith on the part of the people. Our infidel teachers have brought them to doubt whether there be a personal God in the heavens, whether sin is regarded of Him, whether judgment is certain and whether hell is a reality, and the result is not only impenitence but moral pandemonium. In the old day when our fathers stood in the pulpits and in burning words declared "It is appointed unto men once to die, and after that the judgment," their auditors believed them and believed God. Penitence resulted; pentecosts came to pass; regeneration was produced and reform was witnessed. But where now do you find a man weeping over his sins? And when did any new theologian bring his auditors to alarm like that which smote the hearers of President Edwards, lest they had walked so long in the evil way that their feet were on the brink of hell? When Jonah preached "Judgment" in the streets of sin-besotted Ninevah, prince and peasant alike repented and reformed! But a more unalarming proclamation has never reached the ears of men than that which is phrased in the so-called "New Theology." When its sermons are finished sinners applaud the opinions expressed and "proceed further in ungodliness."

THE PHILOSOPHY OF THE STEADFAST.

"Howbeit the firm foundation of God standeth, having this seal, The Lord knoweth them that are his: and, Let every one that nameth the name of the Lord depart from unrighteousness."

That philosophy has three features:

The first is, *an inspired Book.* "The firm foundation of God" is found in that "all Scripture is God-breathed." The law of Moses is a living law. The Song of David is an inspired song. The Gospels of the four writers are a revelation of grace. The Word of the Lord is an end of controversy. The sentences of the Bible are both ancient and modern. Like the sun, it is a long time since they found expression, but their shining is dimmed in nothing. A Hindoo convert, who had carried one Bible until it was worn out, spoke of it as "ancient," and then corrected himself, "I beg pardon, the cover and paper are ancient, but its truths are ever new."

The steadfast have an assured acceptance. "The Lord knoweth them that are his." The names are written in the Lamb's Book of Life. His promise is, "I shall lose not a one." And of the Father he declared, "No man shall pluck them out of his hand." No wonder Isaac Watts wrote:

"Firm as the earth thy gospel stands,
 My Lord, my hope, my trust;
 If I am found in Jesus' hands,
 My soul can ne'er be lost.

His honor is engaged to save
The meanest of his sheep;
All whom his heavenly Father gave,
His hands securely keep.

Nor death nor hell shall e'er remove
His favorites from his breast;
Within the bosom of his love
They must forever rest."

But the third feature of this steadfast philosophy is *an irreproachable conduct.*. "Let every one that nameth the name of the Lord depart from unrighteousness." When all is said that ought to be said in defense of the Old Book against every critic, it remains a fact that the world will never be won by argument. Contend for the faith we should; but its incarnation in our lives is our best contention. A young man was asked what translation of the Bible he liked best, and he answered, "My mother's translation." Whatever men may do with the written epistles of Paul, John, Peter, or James, when they come into contact with those living epistles of Jesus Christ—consistent Christian men and women—who live unselfishly, who devote time to intelligent Scripture research, and who keep themselves unspotted from the world, then they will be most profoundly impressed. No argument can stand against "the Word"—incarnate!

CHAPTER X.

WHAT WILL BE THE RELIGION OF THE FUTURE?

"Other foundation can no man lay than that which is laid, which is Jesus Christ. But if any man build upon the foundation, gold, silver, costly stones, wood, hay, stubble, each man's work shall be made manifest, for the day shall declare it, because it is revealed in fire, and the fire itself shall prove each man's work of what sort it is. If any man's work shall abide which he built thereon, he shall receive a reward. If any man's work shall be burned, he shall suffer loss: but he himself shall be saved, yet so as through fire." (1 Cor. 3:10-15). Schweinfurth's pretentions perished some years since; Sanford is now seldom heard of; Dowie is dead; Mrs. Eddy either dead or alive; and the advocates of the doctrine—"Matter is no part of the reality of existence"—are in court to keep their unreal hands upon their unreal dollars. And yet, of the making of new religions, there is no end. A Cornell University professor, who is not even religious, has lately outlined the coming religion. R. J. Campbell is engaged in a campaign for "The Coming Religion for England." Foster has taken out a patent on "The Plans for Future Faith," and sells each copy of it at $4.20 net. It would not be cheap at half that price. It would seem worth while for those of us who are without a personal axe to grind in the propagation of a new faith, to calmly consider the "Coming Religion," and candidly inquire what it will be like, and what is to be our attitude toward the same.

In investigating the claims of movements, modern and ancient, some of us are convinced that Paul, in the first epistle to the Corinthians, carefully delineated the Coming Religion, describing its foundation, defining its frame, and depicting its finial.

THE FOUNDATION OF THE COMING RELIGION.

"Other foundation can no man lay than that whilh is laid, which is Jesus Christ." The religion which is destined to dominate the future will retain Christ for its foundation: Christ, as the eternal Son of God, Christ as the sinner's substitute and Christ as the solitary Head of the Church.

Christ as the eternal Son of God. At this present moment the real conflict in the theological world rages about the question of Christ. A few years since the good natured Conservatives, who deplored any debate, were saying, "Whatever the Critics take from us, Christ will remain." And even the Critics themselves were then conceding that Christ could not be touched. Within very recent years, however, scores if not hundreds of preachers have risen up to deny the immaculate conception of Jesus, His physical resurrection from the grave, and His ascension to the right hand of God, thereby reducing Him to the level of a mortal man. Some of them reach this conclusion by disputing the authority of the Sacred Scriptures; others by the adoption of the evolutionary theory, and one of the latest, by claiming that Christ appeared to him in person and confessed that He was nothing more than the son of Joseph.

But these are not new movements. The deity of Jesus was disputed by Scribe and Pharisee, explained away by Greek Gnostics, and even derided by the Rationalists of John's day. And yet, the conviction that He was none other than the Son of God has grown, until, beginning with a solitary disciple, it has made conquest of hundreds, thousands, and even of millions of men. The evidence which convinced an uncultured Roman soldier has conquered the logical mind of a Gladstone, and excited the uncompromising testimony of a Webster. This biggest-brained statesman says concerning Jesus, "Every act of His pure and holy life shows that He was the author of truth, the advocate of truth, and the uncompromising sufferer for truth. . . . . Christ was what he professed to be." In some quarters people have questioned whether Tennyson, in his Universalism, made Christ the foundation of all; but listen, while he sings, "What the sun is to that flower Jesus Christ is to my soul." The religion of the future, if it dominate the world, and do men good, will retain as fundamental, Christ the eternal Son of God.

And, Christ as the sinner's substitute. This notion is now inveighed against in some pulpits. Men professing to be abreast of the times, have repudiated the blood, "without the shedding of which there is no remission." To such an extent has this defection from Scriptural teaching occurred that Dr. Augustus H. Strong, on the occasion of his seventieth birthday, sent a message to the students of Rochester Theological Seminary, saying, "I am distressed by some of the common theological tendencies of our times, because I believe them to be false to both science and religion. How men who have ever felt themselves to be lost sinners, and who have once received pardon from their crucified Lord, and Saviour, can thereafter seek to tear down his attributes, deny His deity and atonement, tear from His brow the crown of miracle and sovereignty, relegate Him to the place of a merely moral teacher who influences us only as does Socrates by words spoken across a stretch of ages, passes my comprehension."

Certain pulpit orators, whose audiences are scarcely an inspiration, are saying, "The religion of the future will be ethical," as if the old doctrine of Christ, the sinner's substitute, was not so. To this Campbell Morgan has well answered, "If the great movements under Wesley, Whitfield, Finney, Moody, were not ethical, what were they? They were movements that took hold of vast masses of men and moved them out of back streets into front ones. And if that was not ethical surely nothing can be! Beginning with the regeneration of a man, they changed his environment, and made him a citizen of whom any city might have been proud. That is the true ethical note."

It is a fact which history abundantly illustrates that human progress is by way of human suffering. Some man must perish for the sins of the people. The work of Jesus Christ in this matter is not unique, extraneous, or unnnatural; it was only extensive, effective, sufficient. If Nathan Hale could serve his country by his death why could not Jesus Christ save one of His little worlds by laying down His life in its behalf, so that stricken sinners, looking upon Him, might yet hope, remembering the words of Isaiah, "Surely He hath borne our griefs and carried our sorrows. He was wounded for our transgressions, he was bruised for our iniquities, the chastisement of our peace was upon him, and with his stripes we are healed." The coming religion will hold as fundamental—Christ, the sinner's substitute!

Christ as the solitary Head of the Church! In times past that position has been disputed by the kings of countries characterized by established churches, by the Popes of Romanism; and today such aspirants for office as Mrs. Eddy propose to share it with Him. But it is written, "He is the head of the Church," and some millenniums ago it was prophesied, "He shall have dominion also from sea to sea; and from the river unto the ends of the earth. They that dwell in the wilderness shall bow before him, and his enemies shall lick the dust. The kings of Tarshish and the isles shall render tribute: the kings of Sheba and Seba shall offer gifts, Yea, all the kings shall fall down before him; all nations shall serve him."

Sometime since, in Superior, I listened to Dr. J. Wilbur Chapman speak on "The New Song." He referred to the time when, in Cincinnati, the great chorus of the May Festival of music, appeared, with Patti as soprano, Carey as alto, Theodore Toedt as tenor, Whitney as bass. Just before the Hallelujah chorus there was a death-like stillness over all the throng; then suddenly Whitney sang, "He shall reign forever and ever," and Carey lifted it a little higher; "For He shall reign forever and ever," the tenor carried it almost to the sky, "For He shall reign for ever and ever." Then the sopranos, as if they were inspired, sang, "King of Kings and Lord of Lords." And then, as if the angels were there with their questionings, "How long shall He reign?" With one accord they made reply, "Forever and ever; forever and ever." Then, shouting as the voice of one man, "Hallelujah, Hallelujah, Hallelujah."

The coming religion will put the crown of authority on the same brow that once wore the crown of thorns, and Christ shall be all and over all! "Other foundation can no man lay than that which is laid, which is Jesus Christ."

But having begun with the figure of a building, Paul continues after the same manner. Permit us, therefore, some remarks concerning

THE FRAME OF THE COMING RELIGION.

The design of it is already in the Holy Scriptures. When Moses was about to make the tabernacle, the Lord revealed to him the pattern, including the ark, the altar, and every part of it, from the remotest limits of the outer court, to the sacred holy of holies, and then enjoined, "See thou make it according to the pattern shown to thee in the mount." Those who propose to frame the religion of the future must climb God's holy hill, and attend again and again upon what God has spoken, and they will find not one point of human experience without provision; not one need of body, soul or spirit left in neglect. It is all in the Word!

It may be safely asserted that up to the present there is no other such formula of intelligent faith or basis of beautiful conduct, as that revealed in the old Book. The man who proposes to put that aside and work out his destiny without the assistance of design, will probably discover in crookedness the characteristics of results. His creed will be chaotic and his conduct Quixotic.

The material must come from human service. When you have a good foundation and a well designed frame you have not a house. It is no shield against the wind, no shelter against the storm, no shade against the sun. That framework must be filled in. Paul anticipates this, and talks of our building either with the stable material of "gold, silver, costly stones," or the ephemeral stock of "wood, hay and stubble," declaring "each man's work shall be made manifest, for the day shall declare it, because it is revealed in fire. And the fire itself shall prove each man's work of what sort it is."

There are two classes of religionists in the world, the one made up of people who hold that creed is conduct, believing that if they accept the Bible as inspired from cover to cover they may then "sit and sing themselves away to everlasting bliss," and God will be well satisfied with them. The other class believes that conduct is creed; if you only behave decently it doesn't make much difference what opinions you entertain or propagate. Both are wrong! "As a man thinketh in his heart so is he." A dead creed, however true, is worth nothing; a living creed, if true, will express itself in approved conduct. The true apostle of Jesus says, "I by my works show thee my faith."

The country is full of people who have joined the church, been baptized, and count their religious life complete. At Hull, England, a man went to Campbell Morgan and said, "Do you know, the strangest thing has happened to me?" "What?" said Morgan. "Well, I am a cabinet-maker, and I work at a bench, and another man works by my side. He has worked by my side for five years. I thought I would like to get him to come to some of these meetings, and this morning I summoned up my courage and said to him, 'Charlie, I want you to come along tonight to some meetings we are having down in Wilberforce Hall.' He looked at me and said, 'You don't mean to say you are a Christian?' and I answered, 'Yes, I am.' 'Well,' he said, 'so am I.' Wasn't it funny?" he remarked. "Funny," said Campbell. "Is he here? If so, you both want to get down and start again, you were never regenerated." I believe Campbell was right. The coming religion will never be advanced by the man who "has a name to live but is dead," who says he belongs to Christ but presents Him with no service. I do not know but the churches of this country ought to enter upon a campaign of discipline, and demand of their membership either a response to the call of God, or a retirement from the church of God.

Len Broughton tells the story of an old judge in the mountains of Georgia, characterized by his ignorance of law, but abundance of common sense. Coming into court one morning he found a witness seated in the witness chair with a shawl around him. "You, here to bear testimony?" "Yes." "Put up your right hand." "Judge, my right hand is paralized." "Hold up your left hand then." "The left arm is off." In a spirit of semi-exasperation, he shouted, "Stick up your foot." But the witness answered, "Got them both shot off in the late war." "Then stand on your head, you have got to put up something in this court!" Some stand for the "faith once delivered to the saints," believe the old Book is inspired from cover to cover, and that its statements are scientific. But solemnly, it does not matter how orthodox a man is, if he has nothing to put up in proof of the faith that is in him he is a parasite on the ecclesiastical body, and can only retard the coming of true religion.

The Master Builder is the Holy Spirit. Of Him Jesus said, "When he is come he will guide you into all truth." In building, it is essential to have a leader; a man who combines in one, director and commander. Laggards don't like it. Earnest workmen understand its advantages and gladly acknowledge the supremacy and receive suggestions. Sometimes you will find the master-builder not only a director but a dynamo; he has power in himself and he knows how to impart energy to other people. The Spirit of God is such a director. The church that works under His guidance will neither be crooked nor incompetent. Dr. Gordon says he used to be impressed to see signs as he walked the streets of Boston, which read, "Room for rent, with or without power." The Church of God cannot afford the latter; and it need not, since the Spirit stands ready to administer its affairs.

The individual need not be without power, since the same Spirit is willing to descend upon him and upon her. If you are a clerk in the shop, the Comforter will come there, if you will concede His right and surrender to His reign. If you are the manager of a great corporation He will solve the difficult questions, and show you how to make both your cash and your character tell for Christ. If your are a mother in the home, oppressed by a thousand cares, He will teach you patience, aid you in perseverence, and enrich you with the results. A young man said, 'My mother never made much ado about religion, but as sure as you live she had it. There was something in her life that followed me after she was gone until I was constrained to give my heart to God." Let me affirm it as a fact that in the coming religion men will not be left to themselves to choose their course, think out the proper conduct and build up the proper character. The Spirit of God will administer, and men will marvel at what He has wrought through those who are truly the Lord's own.

The builders have a term which is seldom used in every-day speech; it is "the finial"—"An ornament at the apex of a spire, pinnacle, or the like; a common form in pointed architecture is that of a bud about to open." How the idea fits the apostle's speech, "If any man's work shall abide which he has built thereon he shall receive a reward."

THE FINIAL OF THE COMING RELIGION.

What is in that bud? What is the purpose of it, and what is the promise?

Surely, the holiness of the individual. Paul, in his Epistle to the Ephesians, said, of Christ, "He gave some to be apostles, and some prophets, and some evangelists, and some pastors and teachers, for the perfecting of the saints, unto the work of ministering, unto the building up of the body of Christ, till we all attain unto the unity of the faith, and of the knowledge of the Son of God, unto a full grown man, unto the measure of the stature of the fullness of Christ." (Eph. 4:11-13). That is the meaning of Christ's phrase, "Therefore be ye perfect even as I am perfect"

It refers, not alone to the development of powers, but to separateness from sin. A whole life is also a holy life; hence Christ's command, "Be ye holy."

Compromise with the devil will never make a conquering church; and the professed Christian who does not keep himself unspotted from the world will make no contribution to the coming religion.

Certainly, the happiness of the earth. That is another feature of the finial of the coming religion. True religion is not self-seeking; it is sacrificial. It does not even so much concern itself with personal ecstacy as it does with the happiness of the people. The evidence of Abraham's beautiful character is in the pledge God made him, "In thee shall all the nations of the earth be blessed." The statement that forever ends all quibble concerning Paul's conversion is his cry over unregenerate Israel "I could wish that I myself were anathema from Christ, for my brethren's sake, my kinsmen according to the flesh.' The words of Jesus, as He overlooked Jerusalem, were abundant testimony of His sonship, "Oh Jerusalem, Jerusalem, thou that stonest the prophets, and killest them that are sent unto thee, how often would I have gathered thy children together, as a hen gathers her chickens under her wings, but ye would not!"

More men profess to be Christ's than show any concern for His cause. After consenting to its supreme importance, we let Edison shame us at the point of diligence. Archimedes, we are told, was so absorbed in a problem which he traced upon the sand, that he didn't know of the fall of Syracuse. When he saw a Roman sword drawn on him, he raised his eyes to cry, "Hold your hands a little; only spare my life until I have solved this problem." Beloved, ours is a greater problem—the problem of human happiness, human honor, human redemption. And if the coming religion is to find a finial worthy of it, those of us who name Jesus must give ourselves diligently to the solution of the same.

Finally, that finial involves *a home in heaven*. A Cornell Professor says that "the coming religion will deal in no future! It will address itself to present problems." But you take eternity from the views of men and you destroy their interest in the things of time. Beasts think; their reasoning powers are capable of some cultivation; but they are without hope for the future, and their aspirations never rise above the expression of utter selfishness. Their whole world is one in which every individual is for himself, and the devil gets the hindermost. Thank God, the religion of the future, like the true religion of the past, will present another prospect, will hold out another promise. Jesus has voiced it, "In my Father's house are many mansions; if it were not so I would have told you, for I go to prepare a place for you. And if I go and prepare a place for you I will come again and receive you unto myself, that where I am there ye may be also."

Do you remember how in "Marble Faun" Hawthorne presents Donatello and Miriam as wandering aimlessly along a street at the end of which stood Hilda's tower? He says "There was a light in her high chamber; a light too, at the Virgin's shrine. And the glimmer of these two was the loftiest light beneath the stars. Miriam drew Danatello's arm to make him stop. And while they stood at some distance, looking at Hilda's window, they beheld her approach and throw it open. She leaned far forth and extended her clasped hands towards the sky. "The good, pure, child! She is praying, Donatello," said Miriam, with a kind of simple joy at witnessing the devoutness of her friend. Then her own sin rushed upon her, and she shouted, with the rich strength of her voice, "Pray for us, Hilda; we need it!" Whether Hilda heard and recognized the voice we cannot tell. The window was immediately closed, and her form disappeared from behind the snowy curtain. Miriam felt this to be a token that the cry of her condemned spirit was shut out of heaven. Without hope of it she felt her life to be not worth the living. No religion which despises Heaven will ever command the deep interest in men. In the future, as in the past, that synonym of all conceivable happiness—Heaven—will hold to itself all pure hearts and all righteous hopes. The angels must pity the man, and, even with strong crying and tears, commiserate the woman who misses it!

For Product Safety Concerns and Information please contact our EU
representative GPSR@taylorandfrancis.com
Taylor & Francis Verlag GmbH, Kaufingerstraße 24, 80331 München, Germany

www.ingramcontent.com/pod-product-compliance
Lightning Source LLC
Chambersburg PA
CBHW052107300426
44116CB00010B/1573